T0323603

Cambridge Elements ☰

Elements in Twenty-First Century Music Practice
edited by
Simon Zagorski-Thomas
London College of Music, University of West London

ORIGINAL PIRATE MATERIAL

The Streets and Hip-Hop Transatlantic Exchange

Justin A. Williams
University of Bristol

CAMBRIDGE
UNIVERSITY PRESS

Shaftesbury Road, Cambridge CB2 8EA, United Kingdom

One Liberty Plaza, 20th Floor, New York, NY 10006, USA

477 Williamstown Road, Port Melbourne, VIC 3207, Australia

314–321, 3rd Floor, Plot 3, Splendor Forum, Jasola District Centre,
New Delhi – 110025, India

103 Penang Road, #05-06/07, Visioncrest Commercial, Singapore 238467

Cambridge University Press is part of Cambridge University Press & Assessment,
a department of the University of Cambridge.

We share the University's mission to contribute to society through the pursuit of
education, learning and research at the highest international levels of excellence.

www.cambridge.org
Information on this title: www.cambridge.org/9781009517096

DOI: 10.1017/9781009162616

First published 2024

A catalogue record for this publication is available from the British Library

ISBN 978-1-009-51709-6 Hardback
ISBN 978-1-009-16262-3 Paperback
ISSN 2633-4585 (online)
ISSN 2633-4577 (print)

Cambridge University Press & Assessment has no responsibility for the persistence
or accuracy of URLs for external or third-party internet websites referred to in this
publication and does not guarantee that any content on such websites is, or will
remain, accurate or appropriate.

Original Pirate Material

The Streets and Hip-Hop Transatlantic Exchange

Elements in Twenty-First Century Music Practice

DOI: 10.1017/9781009162616
First published online: November 2024

Justin A. Williams
University of Bristol

Author for correspondence: Justin A. Williams, justin.williams@bristol.ac.uk

Abstract: With his debut album *Original Pirate Material* (2002), Mike Skinner, who recorded under the name The Streets, combined the world of UK dance music with US hip-hop. *Original Pirate Material* is the result of the so-called 'bedroom producer', hybridizing previous forms into something novel. This Element explores a number of themes in this album: white masculinity, the everyday, technology, sampling, hybridity, the Black Atlantic, and US-UK transatlantic relations. It examines the exoticism of Englishness from a US perspective as well as within the wider context of Anglo-American cross influence in post-WWII popular music. Twenty years since the album's release, this Element provides an investigation of the album's content and reception, as an important case study of (postcolonial) hybridity and (English, male) identity.

Keywords: The Streets, UK garage, British hip-hop, hip-hop music, Original Pirate Material

ISBNs: 9781009517096 (HB), 9781009162623 (PB), 9781009162616 (OC)
ISSNs: 2633-4585 (online), 2633-4577 (print)

Contents

Original Pirate Material

<u>Track Listing</u> (and sections in which they are primarily discussed)

1. **Turn the Page** (Section 7)
2. **Has It Come to This?** (Section 1)
3. **Let's Push Things Forward** (Section 2)
4. **Sharp Darts** (Section 5)
5. **Same Old Thing** (Section 4)
6. **Geezers Need Excitement** (Section 6)
7. **It's Too Late** (Section 6)
8. **Too Much Brandy** (Section 6)
9. **Don't Mug Yourself** (Section 6)
10. **Who Got the Funk?** (Section 7)
11. **The Irony of It All** (Section 6)
12. **Weak Become Heroes** (Section 7)
13. **Who Dares Wins** (Section 7)
14. **Stay Positive** (Section 6)

UK Release date: 25 March 2002 (Locked on Records/679 Recordings, double LP and CD)

Japan Release date: 3 July 2002 (Warner Music Japan, CD)

US Release date: 22 October 2002 (Vice Music/Atlantic Records, double LP and CD)

Singles

1. **'Has It Come to This?'** Released: 8 October 2001
2. **'Let's Push Things Forward'** Released: 15 April 2002
3. **'Weak Become Heroes'** Released: 22 July 2002
4. **'Don't Mug Yourself'** Released: 21 October 2002

Charts

UK Albums chart (Reaching number 10 in 2004)
139th in the top 200 hip-hop albums of all time (*Rolling Stone*, 2022)
46th in 100 best albums of all time (*NME*, 2003)

Introduction

This Element analyses an album at the crossroads of early twenty-first-century popular music practice, the debut album from The Streets entitled *Original Pirate Material* (hereafter *OPM*). There is currently little research on this album, or The Streets, or this particular moment in British popular music history.[1] Two decades have passed since the album was released, making the time ripe for a (re-)appraisal of its influences, themes, and its effect on the music industry landscape.

The Streets is the persona of one man who is both MC and producer, Mike Skinner (b. 1979). Originally based in Birmingham, UK, Skinner wrote this album over two years (2000 and 2001) in a number of locations. He recorded tracks in his family home in Birmingham (UK), while living in London with his aunt in Barnet, and eventually in his own accommodation in Brixton where he secured a record deal and finished the album. The earliest tracks were recorded while on a one year working holiday in Australia. Skinner has commented that moving to Australia helped give him a distanced perspective on both England and his desire to make music for a living (Skinner, 2012, pp. 73–74).

The sonic world of the album is one of UK garage mixed with hip-hop influences like the Wu-Tang Clan. There are other musical influences such as ska, reggae, and punk but hip-hop and garage are the overarching styles on the album. Skinner's own vocal delivery is often arhythmic, as if he is telling a story, with what some might consider an exaggerated regional accent. He is not a fast rapper, nor particularly technically skilled. Being a white MC, he has been compared to US rapper Eminem, but they differ in terms of style, rhythmic complexity, and fidelity to autobiographical details in their work.

To this last point, it is important to note that Mike Skinner the artist/song-writer/producer is not to be confused with The Streets the persona. He is not from the streets, nor is he working class. Skinner has always denied that these descriptions are supposed to be him. He says he has come from a 'Barratt

---

[1] One note on my uses of the terms 'UK', 'Britishness', and 'Englishness'. I use the UK for genre in reference to UK garage and UK hip-hop, since more often than not English-based rappers mention the UK as a placeholder for England (Bramwell and Butterworth, 2019). I will use the term British when there is a wider nation-state concern, but I read Skinner's nationalism and localism as part of being English and Englishness, rather than include Scotland, Wales, or Northern Ireland. This issue has been discussed elsewhere (Kumar, 2006; Kumar, 2010), and I have also published on some of the overlapping issues in British, Welsh, Scottish and English rap (Williams, 2021). In short, The Streets as persona deal with England, and while other nations in the UK might find similarities, it is at a time in post-devolution (1997) that England had to start to think about their own identity as a nation (Kumar, 2006). While acknowledging there may be overlap, I prefer to use England and Englishness over Britishness for *OPM*.

Homes' background, rather than the tower block.[2] Though he probably had some hand in popularizing the 'chav' stereotype in the UK, he says he is a storyteller and considers songwriting a craft. It is important, therefore, to not fall into the trap of conflating the artist with their persona. While The Streets do not reflect fidelity to autobiographical detail, many listeners were able to relate to the persona being presented.

It is a global album in many ways, a postcolonial one, and reflective of turn-of-the-century circumstances musically (Section 4), technologically (Section 5), and historically (Sections 2 and 3). It was inspired by hip-hop music, a genre pioneered by Caribbean immigrant to the USA DJ Kool Herc, in New York, a city which was a former Dutch trading post, then English colony (Rose, 1994). Skinner was also inspired by the dance music of London, a global and convivial metropolis (Gilroy, 2004), and formed some of the initial tracks in Australia, a former British colony. Skinner's own origins in the backdrop of bleak postindustrial 1980s–1990s Birmingham are also an important part of the story. *Original Pirate Material* is at once global and yet sounds intimately local. Much of it was recorded in his bedroom, including soundproofing his vocals by recording inside his wardrobe (Skinner, 2012, p. 84). Such a recording technique adds to this sense of intimacy (discussed in Section 5). Like its oxymoronic title, *Original Pirate Material* is full of coexisting binaries and contradictions that are at once ironic but also paint a realistic picture of Skinner's local world.

Methodologically, what follows takes an elemental approach, with each section covering a different theme: pirate radio, the Black Atlantic, transatlantic exchange, intertextuality, technology, lyrical themes of laddism, genre (garage and hip-hop), local notions of Englishness, hybridity, and the mainstreaming of *OPM* and subsequent artists. The primary unit of analysis is the album situated in its socio-historical context, inviting us to explore these different hermeneutic windows. To explore these fully, I draw from critical theory and scholarship around them, with a focus on *OPM*'s lyrics, music, media reception, and Skinner's own writings, in particular, his 2012 autobiography.

I am therefore reliant on Skinner as a reliable narrator in his own story. Without evidence to the contrary, I cannot offer alternatives, but take his writings largely at face value, especially when they help to bolster the thematic material or when discussing compositional process. This Element relies more on journalism and media reception more than some studies may do because the reception of the album in the US and UK and how they differed is an important

---

[2] See online forum for discussion, https://forums.digitalspy.com/discussion/1649102/mike-skinner -streets-chav-or-middle-class.

part of the story. The discursive frames by which the album has been received and discussed are a key part of coding these themes in what follows.

Overall, I argue that Skinner's album is unique in the convergences it reflects: of genre (garage and hip-hop), of the local and the global, of Eurocentric and Afrodiasporic traditions, and a hybrid of localism ('Englishness' or 'little England') and what I call 'Big England' which is a more postcolonial perspective that acknowledges the ramifications of Empire and those global influences still in England. It is a convergence of technologies (Mac and PC; Logic and FruityLoops software), and musical exchange between the UK and US. To the latter, Skinner is part of this tradition of cross-Atlantic influence (discussed in detail in Section 3).

The Streets is, in addition to other things, a performance of white working-class male urban masculinity at the turn of the new century. This is an important detail: Skinner's appropriation of two Afrodisaspuric musical styles is in a long line of such appropriation from the blues to rock and roll to various MC-based genres (e.g. rap, grime). Nor is Skinner the first to invoke pirate radio in his music, or to rap in an English accent. It is worth noting, then, that Skinner was working at a time when pirate radio was thriving in London and in other urban centres, garage and grime were starting to emerge on the scene, and developments in technology (including the internet) were making production easier at home. These elements come together to create an album which reflects the circumstances in which he was recording.

While *OPM* did not adopt stylistic traits of turn-of-the-century US mainstream hip-hop (such as American accents, lyrical topics, or its 1970s funk breakbeat sound worlds), it was trying to show an authentic slice of a regional rap variant regardless of the authenticity of the author. As hip-hop is often focused on 'realness' and on the importance of locality in the genre (McLeod, 1999), this album felt like 'real' England, a social realism which emphasized the everyday rather than, say, the Royal Family. As Kenneth Partridge says in a long review of the album in 2015, *OPM* is a 'perfectly credible regional rap record' in the traditions of Outkast or N.W.A. talking about their localities of Atlanta and Compton respectively.[3]

OPM's localism lets those not privy to England's everyday culture to hear a world previously unknown to them, literally foreign and perhaps even a little weird. For a non-UK listener, hearing The Streets in 2002 represented hip-hop difference as novelty. Skinner's debut album both nuanced and solidified

---

[3] Kenneth Partridge, 'Americans Were Bound to Hate The Streets' *Original Pirate Material' A.V. Club.* 17 February 2015. www.avclub.com/article/americans-were-bound-hate-streets-original-pirate–214890.

particular notions of Englishness, dependent in part on the knowledge of those who listened to it.

For a listener based in the UK, the album may speak to working-class or jobless youths. For others it may simply provide great stories, great music, or both. For better or worse, it also reinforces and complicates stereotypes and archetypes of the so-called 'geezer', the lad, the (usually white) English bloke downing pints and looking for a fight (and a kebab) at the weekend. Upon repeated listening, the album becomes more varied sonically and lyrically than these stereotypes, a mix of the localism of 'Little England' and the wider, postcolonial influences of global cosmopolitanism, of 'Big England' in all its diversity (Williams, 2021, pp. 23–49).

After *Original Pirate Material* was released, the album received generally positive reviews in the UK (along with some confused US-based ones). It was popular with college radio, hipster enclaves, and rose to a level of mainstream popularity on BBC radio and pirate stations. The album helped to encourage record labels to be more bullish about supporting and distributing UK-based artists on a national and international level. So many home-grown musical cultures from England are represented on this album: UK-tinged ska and reggae, UK garage, and even some punk resonances. *Original Pirate Material* presented an edgier-than-Britpop local slice of England, and as ever, these 'local' influences are often a product of the transatlantic and postcolonial relationships of the Black Atlantic rather than simply a hermetically sealed local culture. Like the spirit of the album, the sections that follow provide a multilogue of ideas, hyperlink-style references, and interrogate influences and themes in order to reveal more about *OPM* and its place within English popular culture in addition to its meanings for international audiences.

This Element is divided into three broad parts that correspond roughly with the three words of the album's title. In Part I ('Pirate'), I contextualize the album within the wider history of pirate radio and the importance of this format on the development of British popular music (Section 1). The word pirate also invokes the British Imperial past, when Britannia ruled the waves. I explore Paul Gilroy's notion of a Black Atlantic (1993), a product of the international slave trade (Section 2) as well as the transatlantic 'special relationship' between the US and the UK (Section 3) which also involves a long history of cross-musical influence, such as US minstrel tours to the UK (Pickering, 2008), or Led Zeppelin's rock translation of the blues (Till, 2007). Lastly in section one (Section 4), I take up the more-modern digital piracy aspect of the term (the title's second intended meeting), the 'sample robbery' on *OPM* (referencing a line on The Streets's 'Sharp Darts'), and in hip-hop music more generally.

The second part, entitled 'Material', moves from wider historical contexts to specifics around the construction and composition of the album. I discuss the materials involved in its production (Section 5): the recording equipment, the cultural intermediaries involved, playback formats, and the album's primary lyrical themes (Section 6). I then switch to matters of genre (Section 7) and dissect the two main genres that *OPM* borrows from: hip-hop and garage music. I discuss the development of these two genres and how they fit into *OPM*.

The third and final part is entitled 'Original', the album as a unique convergence of elements, and its importance to the history and the future of British popular music. First, this localized version of UK hip-hop was something non-UK audiences had not heard before, at least those this close to the mainstream. Second, I argue that, paradoxically, the album's hybridity is what makes it successful, and that its specific form of hybridity would have only been possible in a postcolonial Britain (Section 8).

The next section looks at the mainstreaming of other British popular music styles (Section 9). *Original Pirate Material*'s legacy, helped contribute to wider global attention to British artists in the 2000s and beyond. Before concluding, I outline some of the afterlife of the album (Section 10). Twenty years on, this Element provides a thorough investigation of content and delivery, of history, (postcolonial) hybridity, and English working-class white male identity in *OPM*.

PART I: PIRATE

1 Pirate Radio and the Turn of the Twenty-First Century

The pirate related thematic content of *Original Pirate Material* most directly evokes the popularity of pirate radio stations in 1990s Britain. After the string-heavy opening track ('Turn the Page'), Track 2 ('Has It Comes to This?') has a very different feel. There's a looped piano riff with Skinner rapping over the garage beat. The hook of the chorus repeats, 'Original Pirate Material. You're listening to The Streets. Lock down your aerial.' *NME* called it a 'pirate radio call to arms' (Cooper, 2017).

While the 'Lock down' might be a double-voiced reference to *OPM*'s record label (Locked on Records, which itself could be a reference to radio),[4] the aerial explicitly refers to a radio aerial, an antenna transducer which transmits or receives electromagnetic waves. The chorus feels choppy and like a 'talk over' radio DJ, and the track's framing attempts to capture the ethos of a pirate radio broadcast.

---

[4] Locked On Records is a British record label which began in 1996 in London, concentrating on UK garage and grime music (founded by Tarik Nashnush), and is a subsidiary of XL Recordings.

Pirate radio stations have been a highly significant influence on British popular music since at least the 1960s. Alexis Wolton discusses pirate radio in England in the context of the 'land enclosure movement in England' which began largely in the seventeenth century with the consolidation of common land to single ownership, ending its final stages at the turn of the twentieth century. Therefore, wireless communication could be seen as a re-opening of space which now had very fixed ownership on the ground. Those in power, however, did see electromagnetic waves as an extension of land, and in 1927 the International Telecommunications Union divided up, indeed sonically colonized, the physical space amongst their nations. In this sense, pirate radio was a resistant act against the nation-state-based radio monopolies (Wolton, 2011).

The BBC first used the word 'pirated' in the context of unauthorized transmissions of Radio Luxembourg in 1933 (at a frequency not allotted to them by the ITU), but the term started to gain traction in popular parlance in the 1960s alongside a boom in such communications (Wolton, 2011). It is around this time when pirate radio broadcasters attempt to traverse national boundaries by broadcasting from ships. Though the Administrated Radio Conference met in 1959 in Geneva and its delegates passed legislation to prohibit broadcasting stations on ships or aircraft outside national boundaries, radio-ships kept appearing in Europe, including in the UK, such as Radio Caroline, founded March 1964, and Radio Atlanta, founded May 1964. The Marine Broadcast Offences Act was put through Parliament in 1967, effectively ending sea-based pirate radio. Some Radio Caroline DJs had now been offered jobs at the new official popular music station in the UK, BBC Radio 1 (Chapman, 1990; Skues and Kindred, 2014).[5]

Land-based pirate radio in the UK continued into the 1970s and 1980s, examples including Radio Jolly Rodger (based in the West Midlands, founded in 1971) and Radio Enoch (founded in 1978), a politically far-right station that stopped transmitting when the Conservatives came to power in 1979. This era also saw new immigrant communities from the Caribbean being catered to via pirate radio, including Radio Invicta in 1970, the reggae pirate radio station Dread Broadcasting Company (DBC) in London (b. 1980), JFM (b. 1981), London Weekend Radio (b. 1983),[6] and Kiss FM (b. 1985) (Hind and Mosco, 1985; Reynolds, 1998, pp. 273–275). There was a crackdown in the mid-1980s on these stations, and most suffered except for Kiss FM who became a legal entity in 1990. The year 1985 saw the introduction of legal community radio stations in Britain, who like BBC Radio 1 in the

---

[5] Radio Caroline has been mythologized in such films as *The Boat That Rocked* (2009).

[6] A useful history of London pirate radio from teenage bedrooms in 1964 to 1990 (Green Apple Radio) can be found in Hebditch (2015) and a brief summary can also be found in James (2015).

1960s, were able to poach talented DJs from the illegal pirate stations. Reynolds writes of the early 1980s:

> The new pirates broadcast not just from the mainland, but from tower blocks in the heart of the metropolis. As the government closed loopholes in the law and increased the penalties, the illegal stations grew ever more cunning in their struggle to outwit the anti-pirate agents of the Department of Trade and Industry (DTI) . . . By 1989 – 90, there were over 600 stations nationwide, and 60 in the London area alone. And by 1989, a new breed of rave pirates – Sunrise, Centre Force, Dance FM, Fantasy – had joined the ranks of established black dance stations like LWR and Kiss. (Reynolds, 1998, p. 275)

Despite these changes, people found a way to continue pirate radio: Weekend Rush, Kool FM, Rush FM, Pulse, Rinse FM, Eruption, Quest, and others broadcast from council estates in London, as tower blocks have been the pirate modus operandi since the 1980s. Newer technologies such as the portable cellular phone made studio location harder to trace by the Department of Trade and Industry (DTI). These newer stations were often linked to the illegal squat-rave scene. In 1993 BBC Radio 1 fired a number of older DJs and brought in those who had been on the pirate radio stations, including hosts of '1 in the Jungle', 'Fabio and Grooverider', and 'Westwood'. In the 1990s, Rinse FM began as a Jungle pirate in 1994, but diversified stylistically to include garage, and later in the 2000s, grime,[7] dubstep, and UK funky forward. Rinse FM moved online in 2002 (which expanded their audience globally) and went legal with a community radio license in 2011.

The pirate radio that Skinner refers to on his album reflects a 1990s resurgence in pirate radio where first hardcore, then jungle and garage were being broadcast from tower blocks across urban centres in the UK. The year 1992 saw the biggest boom in the history of radio piracy at the time. Simon Reynolds links the 1990s raves, as well as pirate radio, to Hakim Bey's ideas of 'Pirate Utopias' and 'The Temporary Autonomous Zone' (TAZ) (Wolton, 2011). This meaning of piracy engages with the act of theft (and is covered in more detail in Section 4 on sampling and intertextuality), by those who utilize ships dedicated for these purposes.[8] The UK's colonial and Imperial past (when 'Britannia ruled the waves') will become a framework for ideas in Section 3, but it is worth noting how such nautical associations are still very much with us just as the postcolonial is not simply after-colonialism, but that the colonial still lives and breathes

---

[7] For an important study of live London pirate radio sets in the grime context (2001–2005), see Hancox (2018) and de Lacey (2019). For a more comprehensive archive of pirate radio stations by UK region see *The Pirate Archive*, www.thepiratearchive.net/.

[8] For more on the eighteenth-century contexts of social banditry, see Dawdy and Bonni (2012).

here, and its resonances can be felt in systems and institutions, both positively and negatively. Pirate radio boats like Radio Caroline seem to represent a convergence of the two spheres of nautical and airwave piracy.[9]

Pirate radio waves, like pirates on the high seas, transgress man-made borders.[10] It is another way to conceptualize and resist the boundaries and liminal spaces constructed by those in power for their benefit. Skinner himself crosses the borders between musical genre and the track from *OPM* 'Has It Come to This?' becomes an opening statement representative of this new hybrid. These lyrics are a common theme on the album, exploring the mundane or everyday. The lyrics mention the next fight by boxer Mike Tyson, his train route on the London underground, and other rhyming couplets that could be interpreted as stream of consciousness. The rap style has a freestyle feel about it, while referencing specific place names, people, and activities. 'Videos, televisions, 64's PlayStations/Weigh up henry with precision/Few herbs and a bit of Benson/But don't forget the Rizla/ . . . And this is the day in the life of a geezer/ For this ain't a club track/Pull out yer sack and sit back/Whether you white or black'. His references to the music not being a 'club track' but for home listening confirms something that Skinner himself writes in his autobiography: the garage music that influenced him wasn't discovered via clubbing, but through listening at home (with lyrics suggesting while smoking marijuana) or in the car (Skinner, 2012, p. 30). This lends some insight or new perspective on the more discussed rave club cultures of the late 1980s and early 1990s. While club culture is a crucial element to the development of these genres, 1990s British youth like Skinner were also consuming jungle and garage via pirate radio stations.

OPM was released in the UK on 25 March 2002, which was the tail end of the zenith of another form of piracy, illegal downloading of music via file-sharing platforms such as Napster and the numerous other platforms that developed in its wake, including The Pirate Bay. In April 2000, the heavy metal group Metallica sued Napster for copyright infringement and won in March 2001. Dr. Dre and others filed lawsuits subsequently, and the company eventually filed

---

[9] The dominance of national radio broadcasting in the UK at the time was extremely strong compared to other countries such as the USA. UK radio was dominated by the BBC up to this point in the 1960s, with very conservative music policies. The launch of BBC Radio 1 coincided with the forced closing of the pirate ships and resulted in what had been underground or anti-establishment music content becoming integrated in popular culture to a wider extent than previously. Over time, these counter-cultural figures themselves became a somewhat conservative part of the mainstream.

[10] It was one year after *OPM* was released that Disney launched *Pirates of the Caribbean* (2003), which was the first of a successful film franchise starring Johnny Depp, making the pirate archetype even more highly visible in popular culture.

for bankruptcy in 2002. Music piracy contributed to the success of the album through worldwide file sharing at the time.[11]

'Has It Comes to This?' became the album's lead single, reaching number 18 in the UK. The opening of the music video reads 'A Day in the Life' at the top, framing a zooming in shot from above onto Skinner's terraced house and proceeds to go through a day in the life of Skinner (more about the 'everyday' in Section 6). The song has since been put on a list of the forty best garage tracks (1995–2005),[12] and is a good example of a combination of garage beats and Skinner's MC delivery. The single was picked up and put on rotation by Kiss FM, once a pirate, now a legal radio station. Skinner's fusing of UK garage and British hip-hop thus exists in parallel with the legalization of this and other former pirate radio stations, helping this and other styles to have a wider platform. By the end of 'Has It Come to This?' the repeated loop fades out, leaving the soundworld of late 1990s pirate radio and we are about to enter another soundworld entirely.

2 Big England: The Sounds of the Black Atlantic

Track 3 on *OPM* ('Let's Push Things Forward'), the second single from the album, demonstrates sonically what Paul Gilroy calls 'The Black Atlantic.' Gilroy's 1993 book, *The Black Atlantic: Modernity and Double Consciousness*, was a paradigm-shifting contribution to scholarship on the history and art of the Black diaspora. Above all, it expanded the realms of double consciousness of the Black diaspora beyond primarily African American perspectives. Considering the Black Atlantic (including the Caribbean and the UK) as a way to theorize the Black diaspora, he argued that it offered a counterculture to white European modernity. Gilroy's contribution has provided a much-needed Black British counterpoint to more (strategically) essentialized African American-centric work happening in Black Studies departments in the US. His work is necessary in order to grapple with art and culture created in the historical conditions of post-war Britain.

The crucial element of the Black Atlantic we must not forget is that it came about through the trauma and violence of slavery. Modernity and capitalism have unleashed systems which have not only created and perpetuated deep inequalities around cultural constructions of race, but millions of lives have been lost, families separated, and histories erased due to these injustices. The Atlantic Ocean was the site of the flow of goods and enslaved people through

---

[11] An earlier instance of such piracy would be when cassette recordings were heavily criticized by institutions such as the musician union in campaigns such as 'illegal taping is killing music'.

[12] Hannah Moll, 'UK Garage: The 40 Best Tracks of 1995 to 2005' *Mixmag*, 15 March 2019, https://mixmag.net/feature/40-best-uk-garage-tracks-released-90s-00s.

the Middle Passage, which consolidated a cross-cultural nexus under the British Empire. After WWII, labour shortages in the UK provided the impetus to invite thousands of guest workers who were already subjects of Empire to come and work in the UK. Birmingham was one of those key post-WWII hubs of UK immigration:[13] those from former-Empire-then-Commonwealth countries at the time such as India, Pakistan, and the West Indies were encouraged to move to fill the shortages.[14] Those now referred to as the 'Windrush generation', given many migrated on the *Empire Windrush* ship carrying hundreds of passengers from Jamaica in 1948, had an effect not only on demographics but also on culture, including the mixing of music styles. Migrant artists helped to invigorate a British reggae music scene, a ska revival, and reggae-influenced commercially successful acts such as UB40 (from Birmingham). The Coventry scene, not far from Birmingham, is also worth mention, home of 2 Tone Records as well as supporting a thriving rave scene.[15]

These contexts are important for analysing the sounds of 'Let's Push Things Forward'. The track has a slow upbeat-based groove (produced by a synth organ sound) reminiscent of reggae, especially the use of a trombone riff that invokes a harmonic minor scale similar to the anti-industrial dirge 'Ghost Town' (1981) by The Specials.[16] The synthesized bassline is drawn from reggae styles. The chorus is sung by Kevin Mark Trail, a Black British R&B, soul, reggae, and hip-hop artist from West London. The son of Jamaican immigrants, he makes audible and visible the children of the Windrush generation. His chorus lyrics are a critique and a plea to fans and listeners:

> You say that everything sounds the same/
> And then you go buy them/
> There's no excuses, my friend/
> Let's push things forward/

---

[13] This is not to suggest that migrants from the wider Empire only started arriving to Britain after WWII, but reflects a notable surge from the West Indies in particular.

[14] There is the cruel irony worth noting that, while over half a century later after being invited to come, the Theresa May government was set to deny their citizenship and attempt to deport them back to Jamaica.

[15] 2 Tone Records, founded by Jerry Dammers in 1979, was an independent record label which supported music that mixed ska and reggae-influences with some punk and pop. Dammers was a member of the ska revival group The Specials, and the 2 Tone was a reference to the racial integration of some of the groups, including his.

[16] In conversation with Les Back, Gilroy comments: 'One of the tracks is like a radio track led by the trombone ("Let's Push Things Forward") which very clearly registers the power of The Specials, and the "Ghost Town" moment is being recycled. I thought that was interesting: that that had looped back into the soundscape via the kind of Brummy Two-Tone sort of heritage. I don't know how old he is, my guess is, he's about twenty-two, twenty-three. So he wasn't even born then. But that's the language you have to speak in order to be heard now' (Gilroy and Back, 2003, p. 3).

The album makes good on this promise, and Skinner raps, 'this ain't your typical garage joint'. Skinner's first verse opens with:

> This ain't the down, it's the upbeat, make it complete/
> So what's the story, guaranteed accuracy, enhanced CD/
> Latest technology, darts at treble twenty
> /Huge non-recoupable advance, majors be vigilant

His lyrics seem to be referencing the upbeats of the beat in the first instance, followed by a potential reference to Oasis's album *What's the Story, Morning Glory* (1995). Skinner points to the form of the music (CD) followed by referencing a perfect darts score of 180 and a non-recoupable advance from major labels. The braggadocio found in a lot of American hip-hop can be heard in the lines 'This ain't a track, it's a movement, I got the settlement/My frequencies are transient and resonate your eardrums/I make bangers not anthems, leave that to the Artful Dodger'. He is distancing himself from commercially successful garage acts like Artful Dodger, whose music featured sung vocals rather than rap. He comments earlier in the song 'But this ain't your typical garage joint, I make points which hold significance'.

While espousing this message of creating something new, he also reflects on the localism of London: 'Around here we say "birds," not bitches/As London Bridge burns down Brixton's burning up'. He thus makes a rallying cry to a community which seems to be local and translocal. The music video includes Skinner walking through different parts of London, addressing the camera. With what feels like a green screen effect, he traverses in technology-enhanced choppy movements through back streets, suburbs, parks, and the London underground. Kevin Trail is featured in a similar manner visually while he sings the choruses.

Skinner's flow often feels like a stream-of-consciousness narrative at times, and rarely lines up rhythmically to the accompanying beat (at least in a metronomic, percussive sense). Where he goes next in a lyric varies on a number of factors: sometimes there is a clear lyrical connection ('You won't find this on Alta Vista[17]/Cult classic not bestseller'), sometimes he narrates the everyday ('But don't take the shortcut through the subway/It's pay of play, these geezers walk the gangway') including these end rhymes, complete with a number of characters ('geezers', 'backstreet brawlers', 'cornershop crawlers', 'shit-in-a-tray merchants' of the takeaway shop), and includes wordplay like 'Sex, Drugs n' On the Dole'. His Birmingham (or 'Brummie') regional accent comes through in certain instances: 'The hazy fog over the Bullring, the lazy

---

[17] AltaVista was an online search engine founded in 1995, eventually purchased by Yahoo in 2003, and declined into obscurity amidst the rise of Google, ceasing to exist by 2013.

ways the birds sing' in 'Turn the Page', if you listen to the '**a**' vowel in 'hazy', 'lazy' and 'ways' you can hear the vowels associated with the West Midlands accent of England. The glottal stop of Multicultural London English ('have a li**tt**le dance, shall we?') has associations with being in an urban setting, at being 'street level' in The Streets's words. We can also see his penchant for internal rhyme with this line, as well as a specific reference to the Bullring which is now a shopping centre in central Birmingham but has been an import-ant market in the city since at least the Middle Ages. Regarding his rap abilities, Kelefa Sanneh writes, 'Mr. Skinner is a producer and rapper – well, talker more like' (Sanneh, 2006, p. E3). Skinner himself opens the first chapter of his autobiography by saying, 'I'm not a very good rapper. I never have been. And I do know what a good rapper is – there is an objective gold standard – so if you think I am one, you're wrong' (Skinner, 2012, p. 17). The slower pace of talking can help with audibility, especially for lyrics with a lot of wordplay in their delivery. The non-rhythmic element of music of his style as well suggests a spoken style rather than sung or percussive (Krims, 2000).

Perhaps an homage to the braggadocio of 1990s groups like the Wu-Tang Clan and gangsta rap groups, Skinner raps, 'My crew laughs at your rhubarb-and-custard verses' (from 'Turn the Page'),[18] 'You're listening to The Streets, you'll bear witness to some amazing feats' (from 'Has it Come to this?'), or 'Spitting darts faster/ Shut up I'm the driver, you're the passenger/ My brain's superior' (on 'Sharp Darts'). The narrative style has been compared to new wave artists of the early 1980s, Ian Drury,[19] or later from Blur's 'Parklife'. In this track we have the narrative everyday of Britpop, ska horn lines, reggae bassline and grooves, and a smooth chorus, lover's rock style.[20] Such a mix was afforded by the diversity of postcolonial Britain. Visually, the collaboration between Skinner and the Black British Trail (in a music industry which has historically been often racially segregated) is reminiscent of the integrated bands in the UK like The Equals, The Specials, UB40, and Black grime artists

---

[18] There are a few possible readings of 'rhubarb and custard': referencing a children's television show (as Roobarb and Custard) from Skinner's childhood whose theme tune was sampled in an early 1990s rave song, a sweet readily available in sweet shops as well as the name of a kind of ecstasy tablet in the early 1990s. My thanks to James McNally for pointing out these references.

[19] Simon Reynolds in his review of *OPM*, writes, 'Mr. Skinner's chatty, understated delivery is so unusual in hip-hop that he is often compared to English post-punk singers and poets like Ian Dury, John Cooper-Clarke and Terry Hall rather than American rappers' (Reynolds, 2002, p. A28).

[20] Skinner writes, 'My knowledge of reggae got better as I was doing The Streets. 'Let's Push Things Forward' had a ska element, but that came more from a folk memory of The Specials than me knowing anything much about the music that had originally inspired Coventry's finest . . . I've pretty much spent my whole life listening to and making black music and I've always been friends with rappers' (Skinner, 2012, pp. 246–247).

like Roll Deep crew as well as Lethal Bizzle, to the latter has collaborated with white punk artists. It is the postcolonial made audible.

As described in the previous section, the garage and club music of London's Asian and Black communities were best largely served through pirate radio, as they were largely excluded from the legal stations, but pirate radio also opened a level of access for all people to be influenced by a diverse set of musical styles. Pirate radio helped to facilitate the development of a number of subgenres in UK electronic dance music culture, as well as those MC cultures who also draw from such styles, such as grime. This experimentation in opposition to set formulas or genres is reflected in Skinner's line toward the end of 'Let's Push Things Forward': 'Love us or hates us but don't slate us/Don't conform to formulas, pop genres and such'.

The emphasis on newness and looking forward is articulated by Gilroy in his book *After Empire* which has a few pages devoted to The Streets's 'Turn the Page'. Gilroy writes that Skinner has 'explicitly voiced the alternative desire not to recover or repeat the conceits of empire but to shift into a different state of being in the world and "turn the page" of Britain's national history' (Gilroy, 2004, p. 81). Gilroy frames Skinner's recorded persona as part of a forgotten generation, or at least a forgotten demographic in the UK. The success of the album is one indication that the demographic he was said to represent was not forgotten, and of course his whiteness offered him privilege into helping his visibility and popularity. On the other hand, what also added to his success was that his messages were heard and seen by many who could see themselves in them. Gilroy argues additionally that 'Turn the Page', 'recasts the formative, traumatic memory of World War II as a rave. It is also compelling for the way that it refigures an English pastoral consciousness in an urban setting' (Gilroy, 2004, p. 82). In other words, a new national identity could be conceived along multicultural lines, what Gilroy calls conviviality and might be a way forward for reimagining what Britain looks (and sounds) like in the twenty-first century.

3 Transatlantic Relations: Analysing the 'Special Relationship' Musically

Track 5, 'Same Old Thing', samples the first movement of Czech composer Antonín Dvořák's Symphony No. 9 in e minor, subtitled 'From the New World' (Op. 95, B. 178). The symphony could be contextualized in terms of European interest with the United States. Dvořák was inspired by folk melodies from Native American music and African American spirituals as raw material for his symphony, a genre rooted in white European modernity (Shadle, 2021). The 'Same Old Thing' beat loops a string riff sampled from the symphony four times, followed by an orchestral chord which is sustained for over a bar, and then the passage loops repeatedly for the 3-minute, 21-second duration of the song.

The New World Symphony provides a jumping off point to discuss transatlantic musical relations, and for the US-UK relationship more specifically in this section. Post-WWII transnational activity has involved a deep appreciation of American music (Northern Soul), an imitation of it (the blue-eyed soul of Amy Winehouse or Joe Cocker), an appropriation that translates past influences into something new (The Beatles or Led Zeppelin), or an active denial of US influences (for example, in grime). This has, of course, been a reciprocal relationship – on the US side, we could point to the British Invasion, dubstep, and many other styles being the source of fascination by American audiences.

Before the twentieth century, groups like the Fisk Jubilee Singers were visiting Europe; their first concert in England on 6 May 1873 was followed by successful engagements in Scotland, Ireland, and Wales. Their tour raised $50,000 for the construction of Jubilee Hall, which was the first permanent structure on the campus of the Fisk school (Jackson, 2004). Minstrel troupes also toured the UK, including TD Rice who was credited with the 'Jim Crow' character (and the infamous song 'Jump Jim Crow') (Shank, 2001). These Black cultural stereotypes were exported to the UK via these musical performances. UK music hall would have also travelled to the US, which had its parallel with vaudeville entertainment, a mix of songs and comedy skits. The development of recording technologies in the twentieth century made these cross-Atlantic influences even more pertinent.

More famously, The Beatles' love of rhythm and blues was made possible by Liverpool as a port city, which was able to import the latest records from the United States (Davies, 2009). In addition pirate radio stations like Radio Luxembourg and Radio Normandie transmitted American popular music into British homes. The popularity of The Beatles in the US (and the British Invasion in general) is what Andrea Caruso calls the 'paradox of re-colonization' (Caruso, 2013; Till, 2007),[21] and artists like Led Zeppelin have since been sampled by US hip-hop artists creating a further level of cross-influence in composition. Punk music provides another example, its origins in New York City, but swiftly moved to the UK to create something new and exported back to the US and around the world (Covach and Flory, 2018, pp. 381–385). UK garage and offshoots like speed garage were genres that had origins in the US, but were hybrid forms between US garage and UK jungle/drum and bass, very much becoming its own thing in the UK.

---

[21] For a broader study of European-American relations, see Meyer et al. (2008).

In terms of hip-hop specifically, early pioneers in the UK have discussed how they started rapping in American accents, and at a certain point started to rap in their own regional UK accents. Rodney P of London Posse for example, has stated that it was a visit to New York City that helped him to realize that his own accent was valued and considered interesting by those outside of his home country.[22] It was this period in the late 1980s that hip-hop in the UK started to find its own voice, producing offshoots such as Bristol's trip-hop (Massive Attack, Portishead), and in the 1990s artists like Blak Twang, Roots Manuva, TY, and rappers later associated with Low Life Records, such as Jehst, Skinnyman, and Task Force. While trip-hop reached global attention, UK hip-hop was still very much an underground form, eclipsed by Britpop and electronic music artists like Chemical Brothers and The Prodigy. Garage music of groups like So Solid Crew started to reach mainstream success around 2001, a proto-grime music as grime was coming from the underground into its own early moments of success (Dizzee Rascal's Mercury Prize winning *Boy in Da Corner* from 2003 was a watershed moment).

When *Original Pirate Material* was released, UK listeners could identify the garage influences (and understood the accent and slang), but it took some time for the US to have an appropriate frame to identify and understand Skinner's project. Comparisons were initially made with Eminem in *Rolling Stone* and in *The New York Times* (Michel, 2006). Eminem was the first successful white rapper who reached a high level of credibility within the wider hip-hop community, in part by touting his poor, working-class background from the other side of the tracks in Detroit, Michigan, as a sign of sincerity and authenticity. Unlike Eminem, however, Skinner was not from a lower-class background, arguably exaggerating his accent to perform localism in ways that feel more UK-specific.[23]

It took time for US critics to understand Skinner's brand of 'hip-hop'. Chuck Klosterman writes, 'his debut record, Original Pirate Material, sold slightly more than 100,000 copies in the United States, but it has been dubbed the first transcendent hip-hop album ever to emerge from England – which is kind of like being dubbed the sexiest female at a hobbit convention' (Klosterman, 2003, p. M24). Rob Mitchum wrote the following review of the album:

> It should come as no surprise that the British, notorious for chewing on our music before spitting it back over the Atlantic in a shiny, new form, have also turned their sun-starved faces to the arena of hip-hop. There's just one small

---

[22] Rodney P, 'Hip-Hop Saved My Life' Podcast, Romesh Ranganathan, Ep. 63. 31 Oct. 2018.
[23] Eminem's fourth studio album *The Eminem Show* was released in 2002 and debuted at number one on the *Billboard 200*, and generated sales of three million units in the first four weeks. This is the milieu in which Skinner's album was released and received (more on Eminem and Skinner in Section 6).

problem: simply put, British accents just don't sound particularly right in the context of syncopated rap-speech. To put my tweed linguistics jacket on, the American tendency to cheat on pronunciation fits in perfectly with the wordplay of hip-hop, while the stubborn British habit of perfectly enunciating every syllable makes things sound rather, well, formal . . . Which is why the first time you put on *Original Pirate Material*, you might find it awfully hysterical – especially if the name had you assuming it was going to be another Strokesian garage act. The giggles will eventually give way to a bit of discomfort at the slightly awkward delivery– the words here are jammed into measures like an overstuffed couch. (Mitchum, 2002)

Skinner's delivery was commented on in contrast to garage MCs or hip-hop infused American R&B: 'instead of hyper-speed ragga chatting or candy-coated divas (or both), listeners heard banging tracks hosted by a strangely conversational bloke with a mock cockney accent and a half-singing, half-rapping delivery' (Bush). John Bush continues his review, 'True, describing his delivery as rapping would be giving an undeserved compliment (you surely wouldn't hear any American rappers dropping bombs like this line: "I wholeheartedly agree with your viewpoint")', and concludes by saying positively that it is one of the better garage albums in that its shelf life goes beyond six months (Bush). He also points to a particular lineage of artists when he writes that Skinner is 'the latest dot along a line connecting quintessentially British musicians/humorists/social critics Nöel Coward, the Kinks, Ian Dury, the Jam, the Specials, and Happy Mondays' (Bush). Jon Caramanica calls Skinner the 'pub hooligan Marshall Mathers' and points out that he 'could be the most gifted rapper London has ever produced, except that he doesn't really rap–he pontificates, spins spoken-word yarns, and kicks running commentary' (Caramanica, 2003). One reviewer insensitively describes Skinner's flow as having 'an inherent verbal handicap' (Mitchum, 2002). Other reviewers called it 'inaccessible': 'The Streets' debut is an electronica album, a cultural artefact, a rap release, a poetry slam, and an anthropology lesson all-in-one. It's also the most artfully done, but ultimately inaccessible, mainstream album in years' (Simpson, 2003).

Simon Reynolds's review of *OPM* also touches on these relations between the two countries very directly:

> The British have always had a flair for taking black American music, giving it twist and then exporting it back, stylishly repackaged. Blues R&B, soul, funk, disco, house – each in turn has been the source music for a series of British invasions of the American pop mainstream. Yet, despite years of trying, this native genius for appropriation has spectacularly failed in one area: hip-hop. From late-80's contenders like Ruthless Rap Assassins to 90's groups like the Brotherhood, British rappers have not made much impression in hip-hop's homeland. (Reynolds, 2002, P. A28)

Reynolds goes on to cite various opinions on how the British 'patter' isn't natural for the American-style flows of US rap. Counter to this, Skinner has 'taken the idioms and cadences of colloquial English and made them work as hip-hop' (Reynolds, 2002, p. A28). His review was published a week before the album was released in the US (October 2002), and posits that the album could do well in the US for the same reason that US rap does well in the UK, it provides an exotic fantasy for listeners across the pond. Ultimately, this did happen to an extent with white male hipster communities (including US college radio) who found the slice of English life to be sufficiently exotic.

Skinner writes candidly about his first world tours and his being surprised at the predominantly white male hipster audiences in front of him. He thought it would start out as a favourite with 'normal people' (Skinner, 2012, p. 94) and go from there, but he says that because it sounded different, it was popular with those who always gravitate toward the new:

> When it [OPM] first came out, all the people I was meeting in the exciting new places I was going to – Berlin, New York, San Francisco – seemed to be the kind of people who were into the new thing as a kind of reflex. Because, for my first album at least, 'the new thing' is what I was. (Skinner, 2012, p. 94)[24]

He also writes in his autobiography, *The Story of The Streets*, that

> I didn't want to make strange hipster music, I wanted to make a record that would instantly make sense to a certain set of people. But because I wasn't really the type of person I was trying to communicate with – it was the people I'd been working with before (the ones who ended up getting very pissed off with me) who were actually the type of person – the audience I'd intended *Original Pirate Material* to be for didn't really get it. (Skinner, 2012, p. 88)

In addition to the perceived economic stability and male gender of these hipsters, there was also a racial element to this demographic and the style of music Skinner was trying to make. Skinner has stated in interviews that his circle of friends are multicultural, reflective of British urban youth in cities like London and Birmingham. But in terms of mainstreaming his music, he sees a similarity with those who took the blues and became big fans and appropriators:

> The Streets was not about being from The Streets – that was kind of the point of it. And that's why the people *Original Pirate Material* spoke to most clearly all seemed to live in Shoreditch and Williamsburg and lots of other

---

[24] Skinner writes, 'If you look at Original Pirate Material, in my head that album was going to be quite a generic thing, the first of an inevitable series of British hip-hop records that would be made using garage beats. But what it actually ended up being was quite characterful and odd' (Skinner, 2012, p. 88).

places I would never previously have imagined myself hanging out in. I don't think there's anything wrong with that, either. I guess there's another blues parallel here: how many black people do you actually see in the crowd when BB King plays at Glastonbury? (Skinner, 2012, pp. 88–89)

Skinner's comment harkens back to the UK interest in African American music, and a wider history of white middle-class interest in these genres. What this shows, however, is that these processes continue into the twenty-first century. In terms of Skinner's persona of The Streets, he initially wanted to be an anonymous artist, but he realized he had to do gigs and music videos. His first gigs as The Streets were at the Reading and Leeds festivals on the August bank holiday weekend of 2002 and he came to terms with the fact he was rapping a persona that wasn't himself. However, person and persona were becoming conflated in his artistic reception.

In contrast to those who were confused or dismissive of the debut album, those who understood *OPM*'s *sonic framework* were those who were more familiar with garage music. Counter to Sanneh's description of Skinner as a 'talker' rather than a 'rapper' mentioned in the previous section, UK journalists understood the garage contexts for his MCing as John Robinson dubbed Skinner the 'New, brummie voice of Garage' (Robinson, 2005). *Entertainment Weekly*'s review wrote, 'By adding grit and gutter-savvy humor, Skinner also takes U.K. garage to a new level, making for the year's most striking debut' (Entertainment Weekly). The *Village Voice* wrote, 'Original Pirate Material is England's first great hip-hop record mostly because it isn't a hip-hop record. It's hard to say exactly what it is' (Village Voice). Whether it was an exoticism that listeners struggled to understand but were interested in, or thought of a garage MC with roots reminiscent of the great British storytellers (including The Kinks, Sex Pistols, and John Cooper Clarke), Skinner's brand of popular music was novel. It brought hip-hop late to the table of Britpop, adopting the narrative prose of Blur's 'Parklife', alongside a Britpop-esque 'mockney' accent that many critics of the *OPM* commented on as Skinner trying to hide his West Midlands origins (Skinner, 2012, p. 86). Contrasting with the Black London Caribbean-influenced accents of the likes of So Solid Crew, who actually emerged from the Pirate Radio scene, it suggested a style in which UK rappers could achieve commercial success internationally (and in the large US market in particular), free from the restraints of imitation of American hip-hop voices.

4 Sample Robbery

'Sharp Darts', track 4 on the album, features a slightly harder hip-hop beat compared to other tracks on the album, and provides a vehicle for The Streets's bragging about his lyrical prowess. He compares his lyrics to darts, proclaiming 'your beats are inferior', punctuating his chorus addressed to his rival(s): 'Do you understand or do you need an interpreter?' He threatens to rob his opponent by way of sampling them. The end of the second verse says, 'One day I hope to earn some hard royalties from a bit of sample robbery/Hook burglary, noise thievery or wholesale piracy/ So watch your back, I'm inclined to sample/ I'll dismantle and make you all examples.'

Digital sampling has been important to hip-hop aesthetics since the mid-to-late 1980s. It is but one of many forms of musical intertextuality, part of a vast web of references, citation, homage, and quotation that comprises a core component of the genre (Williams, 2013). Hip-Hop is not only a musical genre, nor is it simply the oft-cited 'four elements' of graffiti, breakdancing, MCing and DJing, but it is an approach to performance and an even wider approach to aesthetics in general (Williams, 2015, p. 1). This affects not only music, dancing and visual arts, but cinema, fashion, language, and many other facets of culture. Rather than espouse a modernist impulse to celebrate the new or original, hip-hop openly celebrates past influences. Not only is hip-hop music highly intertextual in lyrics, their delivery, and in their beats (Williams, 2013), but its intertextuality is overtly performed. In other words, hip-hop's reference of past material is pointed to or highlighted in a number of ways. The Dvorak sample discussed in the previous section is but type of explicitly borrowing from the past, and one of the few (if not the only) digital samples on the album. You can hear the splicing in the loop, the ruptures are opened and audible, the inner working parts are shown on display.

With regard to the legality of using material through digital sampling, in many ways, Skinner's drawing from hip-hop aesthetics and borrowing practices is quite risk-averse as he didn't have to clear many samples for the album. We have his own audio loops, and potential string samples which might have gone under the radar, or are 'performed samples' (made to sound sampled, but were created by the producer; Exarchos, 2024). And the FruityLoops and Logic software he used for the album include material that is copyright free. The lack of sample material, however, provides an opportunity to investigate the other types of musical borrowing found within the album. While not a comprehensive taxonomy, Table 1 shows some of the different types of intertextual practices in the lyrics and their delivery ('flow') and the sonic elements that comprise the 'beat' in a given track on the album:

While we can point to a web of influences for The Streets, Skinner is the strong authorial presence behind the music. He collaborates with other vocalists (such as Kevin Mark Trail), and his autobiography alludes to

Table 1 Non-exhaustive Types of Musical Borrowing in *OPM*

Intertextuality Type	Found in	Example
Digital Sampling	Beat	Dvořák in 'Same Old Thing'
Stylistic allusion	Beat	2-tone/ska in 'Let's Push Things Forward'
Lyrical references	Flow	Video games, cars, shoes, radio, alcohol, food
Interpellation (harmonic progression)	Beat	'Let it Be' chord progression for 'Never Been to Church' (not on *OPM* but on the 2006 album *The Hardest Way to Make an Easy Living*)
Lyrical Signifyin(g)	Flow	Wordplay, humour, double-voiced utterances, simile, metaphor, irony

people he worked with in Birmingham who seem to go missing in the story after his move to London, angry at him for not giving them more credit. Skinner writes:

> There were two criticisms of Original Pirate Material that seemed quite serious at the time. One was that by effectively making The Streets a solo project and leaving behind the people I'd previously been working with I somehow almost stole their souls. The other was that I was some kind of West Midlands mockney wannabe, pretending to be a Londoner even though I actually came from Birmingham. Like a lot of unfair accusations, both of these charges contained an element of truth that somehow got twisted. (Skinner, 2012, p. 86)

While it is difficult to unpack this type of collaborative authorship (we hear Skinner's side mostly in books, articles, and journalism), the fact he's produced five full-length albums which are stylistically similar (relatively speaking) suggests that he is the principal creative force behind The Streets in both beat and flow. Furthermore, to have the MC and producer/DJ be the same person was rare in UK garage (and hip-hop to a lesser extent) at the time. This could be down to the party origins of the genres, which consisted of a DJ on turntables and one or more MCs in a live music setting. The laptop-based bedroom producer aspect of Skinner's work helps make an integration between the two elements possible. Nothing is ever completely sole authored, given the range of influences that helped to shape Skinner's creative process, and could be considered a collaboration in an intertextual sense.

In terms of his own compositional process, Skinner admits to extensive use of songwriting and screenwriting 'how to' manuals, especially in the albums written after *OPM*.[25] He also took a screenwriting course in London between his third and fourth albums. Skinner suggests that everything necessarily builds upon previous ideas in the title of The Streets's fourth album *Everything Is Borrowed*. This means that in addition to digital sampling, lyrical references, genre hybridity, and wordplay, there are a number of tropes and narrative ideas utilized in his compositional output. *Original Pirate Material* has narrative themes, especially the middle tracks on the album, but are less developed than that of his later albums (the *OPM* tracks 'Geezers Need Excitement' and 'Stay Positive' might be notable exceptions), especially the narrative through-line of his second album *A Grand Don't Come for Free* (2004).

In addition to digital sampling, the album has multiple instances of quotation – lyrical and in beat, stylistic allusion, wordplay, rhyme, simile, metaphor, humour, and braggadocio as found globally in hip-hop. Lines like 'Give me a jungle, a garage beat, and admit defeat' from 'Turn the page' show a level of bragging and one-upmanship. Furthermore, the line 'I shake and reveal stage tricks like Jimi Hendrix' ('Turn the Page') combines bragging and simile with reference to a famous African American musician known for pushing the boundaries of his instrument and musical genre. Insult-laden bragging in rap derives from the African American tradition of playing 'the dozens'. The dozens refers specifically to a game where two people insult one another until one gives up. The term has its origins in the New Orleans slave trade, where enslaved people who were considered less valuable were grouped into a dozen to be sold at a low price. Therefore, to be one of the dozens was an insult (Wald, 2012). Another example of insult lyrics is in 'Sharp Darts': 'This one's fat like yer mother/ Contains enough calories/Resonating all your favourite frequencies.' A use of simile as part of the narrative flow can be heard in 'Geezers need Excitement': 'He looks like a Cheshire cat, almost falls down, dour frowns/And Superman eye-lasers don't even register'.

UK-specific wordplay present includes a variation on the process of truncation used in cockney rhyming slang, which has its origins in the East End of London. For Skinner, he uses the actual word rather than a rhyming substitution. One example is when Skinner refers to brandy as 'Marlons' (as in Marlon Brando) in the song 'Too Much Brandy', or the 'Weighing up Henry' line in 'Has it Come to this?' as Henry refers to Henry VIII, hence an eighth of an ounce of cannabis, or approximately 3.5 grams. Sometimes there is elision or synecdoche, such as when he raps, 'When my life went pear, she'd been there with a thick stare' ('It's too late'). Here the

---

[25] 'I've never paid much attention in English lessons in school, but in the months and years after that first Reading Festival I devoured pretty much every book there is to buy on songwriting' (Skinner, 2012, p. 111).

'pear' refers to the idiom of something 'going pear-shaped' or not quite according to plan.

Skinner might change the punchline of an expected idiom or phrase as in 'Sex drugs and on the dole' or 'Lock, stock and two fat fucks backin him up' ('Geezers need excitement'): the latter an intertextual reference to the Guy Ritchie film *Lock, Stock, and Two Smoking Barrels* (1998). The internal rhyme of 'Amsterdam ain't a nice place off your face/We enter the race' ('Too Much Brandy') demonstrates one aspect of rap's poetics. 'So you tell your mates you could have him anyway, to look geez, but heez [he's] a shady fuck' ('Geezers need excitement') foreground the sounds of words, reminiscent of Henry Louis Gates's concept of Signifyin(g) where the signifier is fore-grounded for its own sake (Gates Jr., 1988). As we will see in Section 6, many of these lyrical references are to emphasize the localism of English everyday life of this persona, combining with accent to solidify a particular type of Englishness being performed.

There is humour and irony at play as well, such as 'We met through a shared view, she loved me and I did too' ('It's too Late'), again perhaps another inversion of expectation. The two most humorous songs on the album are perhaps 'Don't Mug Yourself', involving a friend making sure that Skinner's persona doesn't get too involved with a woman he just met, and 'The Irony of It All' which tells of a debate between a pot smoker and heavy pint drinker. The lyrics discuss that cannabis is technically illegal while alcohol is legal, yet alcohol causes more deaths and costs in hospital Accident and Emergency units ('My Name's Terry and I'm a law abider vs. my name's Tim and I'm a criminal'). The lyrics contrast level of harm with the very different social stigma attached to these forms of consumption. But through characterizing this debate through stereotypes, there is a level of humour infused in this political debate.

Lastly, Skinner uses frequent lyrical references to video games (64s, PlayStation in 'Has it Come to this?'; Gran Turismo ('The Irony of It All'), cars (SR Nova in 'Has it Come to this?'), public transport (the London under-ground in 'Let's Push Things Forward' and 'Who Dares Wins'), shoes (Nike, in 'Who Dares Wins'), radio stations (Lock On 102.6), alcoholic drinks ('Too Much Brandy', Smirnoff Ice rounds in 'Geezers Need excitement'; Kronenberg lager in 'Whose Got the Funk' and 'Who Dares Wins'; Carling lager in 'The Irony of it All'), drugs (E in 'Weak Become Heroes'; marijuana in 'The Irony of it All'), food ('carry on cutting the finest cuts of chicken from the big spinning stick' in 'Geezers Need Excitement', 'full English [breakfast] with plenty of fried tomato' in 'Don't Mug Yourself'; 'Grab something to eat, Maccy D's or KFC' in 'Weak Become Heroes' and 'Same Chinese take-away selling shit in a tray' from the same song). The SR nova, KFC, Kronenberg, and other references are signifiers of male urban youth at the time, and pointing to a non-elite culture. 'Weak Become Heroes' shouts out a number of DJs that were influential for Skinner, a citational process is also common in hip-hop. Overall, the selection of words is characteristic of British cultural references, and combined with the accent in which they are presented, this creates a very specific overall effect.

This vast web of references and musical borrowing practices in beat and flow, like hip-hop itself, is often grounded in African-based practices (many of which, like in garage and hip-hop, were direct influences on Skinner), but the late capitalist frameworks of the popular music industry sometimes compli-cates or hinders such practices. Ownership of musical material has had a long and complex history. A number of high-profile sampling lawsuits in the early 1990s (involving De La Soul, Biz Markie, and others) meant that those who could afford to sample music had to clear the rights. This affected the landscape of hip-hop creativity (Williams, 2015, p. 208). Skinner recounts in his autobiography that he had to include a co-writing credit on his music when Sir Paul McCartney sued him over his alleged pastiche of 'Let It Be' for the song 'Never Went to Church' (from his 2006 album *The Hardest Way to Make an Easy Living*), which has a similar chord progression. Skinner writes of songwriting:

> There's a great deal of self-delusion in songwriting. A lot of people write a song quite quickly and then they feel like it would be sacrilege to alter it. I suppose they like the idea of saying 'it just came to me'. To be fair, it is sometimes possible to come up with something that's going to be around for ages in the time it takes to boil a kettle, but that's not the way it usually works. I couldn't put the process into better words than those of the man who up until the fourth Streets album was the only songwriter I had collaborated with on The Streets. His name was Paul McCartney (by way of a lawsuit over 'Never Went to Church') and the words were 'take a bad song and make it better. (Skinner, 2012, p. 8)

As many copyright infringement cases are settled out of court for non-disclosed amounts of money, it is often difficult studying them. Researchers interested in the details of cases, on what grounds cases win or lose, rely on testimonies from forensic musicologists (who need to prove or disprove similarities). Amounts awarded may be hidden leaving scholars left in the dark. This approach to copyright often ignores more collective forms of music making, based on oral tradition and diverging ideas of ownership.

Skinner sees songwriting as a craft and as something that can be taught and learnt rather than 'divinely decreed' (Skinner, 2012, p. 116). In the Element's next section, we shift to the album's materiality: the technology involved in its composition, its format, lyrical topics, and genres utilized.

PART II: MATERIAL

5 Technology and Production

Original Pirate Material was recorded over two years (2000 and 2001) in a number of locations: Skinner's family home in Birmingham, UK; in Australia during a working year abroad; while living in London with his aunt in Barnet; and eventually in his own flat in Brixton where he secured a record deal and finished the album.[26] This section investigates the materiality of the recording process, both the technology used to record *OPM*, the importance of format, and how the album and its tracks circulated at the turn of the century.

When Skinner moved to Australia in 1999, he was working in bars in the evening and carrying out a second job in Y2K compliance in the daytime. The Millennium Bug failed to materialize into the disastrous global collapse that some thought it would create, but, as Skinner notes, his work to fix the bug provided the income for his IBM laptop PC ThinkPad on which he wrote many of the songs on the album. He wrote the album's last track, 'Stay Positive', in the flat in Darlinghurst next to King's Cross in Sydney. He recounts in his autobiography the recording equipment he brought to Australia:

> I didn't completely leave music behind when I went to Australia . . . I had [my gear] all quite expertly packed, and I have special padlocks for it. There was an SP808, which is an old zip-disc sampler that's a really cool hybrid between a sampler and a recorder, a Zoom sampling drum machine, and I also took a microphone –an AKG C1000. (Skinner, 2012, p. 70)

His experience in Australia also helped him to look at Englishness and his own upbringing with a new distanced perspective. When he returned to Birmingham, he came up with the idea of The Streets as a persona, and continued trying to write dance music and other hip-hop-inflected music to shop to labels. 'Has It Come to This?' was written while living in a shared house in Brixton (Skinner, 2012, p. 65), and got the attention of Andy Lewis at Locked On Records (a subsidiary of XL Recordings), a label which specialized in UK garage and, later, grime.

---

[26] 'It took me a year to finish Original Pirate Material. After six months living in Barnet, I popped back to Birmingham for a bit, then got my own room in Brixton, and inside that shared house in SW9 was where the bulk of the album got done. I already had 'Stay Positive' and 'Has it Come to this?'; 'Let's push things forward, don't mug yourself, turn the page, too much brandy and 'It's too late' were all put together on my ThinkPad in the room I'd rented from this really nice Jamaican guy and his wife, who was a Finnish yoga teacher' (Skinner, 2012, p. 83).

We should contextualize Skinner's work under the phenomenon of the laptop-based bedroom producer (Glynn, 2020) and the DIY impulse which was flourishing at this time (Bell, 2014). The early 1980s introduced cassette multi-track recorders which were used in amateur home studios. It was the Digital Audio Workstation, or DAW, computer software which allowed in the 1990s for professional standard digital recordings to be produced in people's homes. The development of the internet alongside DAWs was an important companion to the rise of home studio technologies.

The DAW software that he initially used for the album was FruityLoops, software which was developed in 1997 and consisted of a four-channel step sequencer with a 127-note musical instrument digital interface (MIDI) bank to select drum sounds and patterns. Reflecting its name, it afforded a loop-based style of composition which was relatively user-friendly, and the rise of the software, as Mike D'Errico notes, paralleled the 'viral spread and Wild West nature of internet culture in the late 1990s and early 2000s' (D'Errico, 2022, p. 26).[27] The software was often 'cracked' and people would use an illegally downloaded copy, alongside the declining cost of home computers at the time meant more people had access to production software (Bramwell, 2015, p. 18). FruityLoops was only available for PC use at the time, and when Skinner got his first Mac laptop during the latter stages of *OPM* recording, he moved over to Logic Pro to create beats (software which he says he still uses), also very loop-based production software which was acquired by Apple in 2002.

Skinner spent his last six months of album composition sequestered in his Brixton flat. He was using an emptied-out wardrobe as his vocal booth, and the home-made studio had duvets and a mattress to control the acoustics of the space. Thick duvets were used to provide dead studio-like acoustics (Skinner, 2012, p. 84).

Skinner saw the benefits of home recording as the ability both to have unlimited time and so that he could retain control of every element of the process (Skinner, 2012, p. 85). The independent process allows less interference from other intermediaries, allowing musicians to capture and distribute new ideas more quickly (Waltzer, 2021; Kaloterakis, 2013; De Carvalho, 2012). Some interpreted the sounds as more home-grown given that they came from the bedroom, as artist Clare Maguire writes:

---

[27] FruityLoops was later named *FL Studio* and has gone through over twenty versions of the software. It has been used by Soulja Boy, Sonny Digital, 9th Wonder, Wiley, Jhalil Beats, Kanye West, Deadmau5, and many others (Adams, 2019, p. 439; D'Errico, 2022; Jackson, 2015). For more on the democratization of music production through DAW technologies, see Strachan (2017).

> He was from Birmingham as well [as I am] so the album really resonated with
> me. He spoke like the everyday man, which was what my Dad was like. The
> sounds he was using in the production were like what you'd hear walking
> through Birmingham – garage music that sounded like people had made it in
> their bedrooms. (Quoted in Myers, 2017)

There was also another reason to work at home on a high-quality laptop, and that
was due to Skinner's epilepsy. According to him, the reason Skinner made his
first album on a laptop 'was because the screens they had were the first ones
I could look at for long periods. So I was an early adopter, but it was more for
medical reasons' (Skinner, 2012, p. 258). Harkness (2014) has theorized the
professional recording studio as a symbolic and venerated space in hip-hop
culture; Skinner describes it as a space in which socialization is important.[28]
While this may be the case, laptop-based production allowed for producers with
a diverse set of abilities to create in their own timeframes under their own
unique circumstances.

Echoing discussions of piracy from Section 1, it is worth mentioning that
DAW software in this era was often illegally downloaded rather than purchased,
which facilitated free access to music production software for bedroom producers who could not afford the several hundred-pound prices. Though Skinner
does not mention this in his own compositional practices (he does admit to
downloading music on Napster), it is yet another element of musical 'piracy'.
The piracy of *OPM* may be most directly referring to pirate radio, but also
references a range of other emergingly piratical elements of the music industry,
including access to the recording and production software that allowed the
bedroom producer to usher in a new era of DIY music making at the turn of
the twenty-first century.

While the bedroom studio can be mythologized as the laboratory of the sole-
creator, there is a wider network of intermediaries as part of any creative
endeavour. The making of this album is a story of multiple spaces, places, and
geographies: of Birmingham, Sydney, and London and the German-born,
London-based photographer of the album cover, Rut Blees Luxemburg. The
record contract for *OPM* went through Locked On Records, but was the first
release on its new label 679 records, which was run by Nick Worthington who
was Skinner's A&R man from Locked On. This was an independent label that
had a deal with major label Warner Brothers for album distribution.

---

[28] 'Until the people who are making it start to have a bit of success and become DJs, house music is
essentially a solitary business – it's just guys in bedrooms, really. But with rap, there are always
a lot of people about, and that's one of the things I liked most about it.' Skinner, *Story of the
Streets*, 56.

The album was released on both CD and vinyl in March 2002 in the UK and October 2002 in the US, with four official singles released between October 2001 and October 2002. According to the British Phonographic Industry (BPI), *OPM* is certified 2 x platinum in the UK, an index that marks platinum sales as 300,000, so *OPM* sold over 600,000 total units in that country alone. In the 1990s, as CDs started to take more of the market share, artists and bands were able to incorporate more digital technologies in their recording process, and perhaps extend the idea of the concept album in new directions. Dai Griffiths (2004) makes a specific case for the CD album as a specific type of music album, with echoes of previous indebtedness to the album of the vinyl era, but also offering something new.[29] The longer-potential length of the CD album is one feature, as well as the continuous flow (not having to turn sides of a record). Griffiths also points to an emphasis on the middle tracks of an album, while bunching up of singles at the start of an album. At 47 minutes, 24 seconds total length, *OPM* is not a tremendously long album, but it does follow a journey over fourteen tracks:[30] a mix of singles early on (tracks 2 and 3), followed by normal song-length tracks peppered with two tracks under two minutes (10, 'Who Got the Funk?' and 4, 'Sharp Darts'), one under a minute (13, 'Who Dares Wins'), followed by the final track at longer than six minutes (14, 'Stay Positive'). 'Weak Become Heroes' (track 12), an ode to the glory days of house music, is slightly longer than traditional single-length at 5 min, 35 seconds. The variety in track lengths does suggest it is tailored to listening in one session on a home stereo, CD Walkman, or in the car for those who had access to such playback technologies at the time.

While the tracks can be listened to as songs in any order, and *OPM* is not a 'concept album' in the traditional sense,[31] I argue that the album was a common enough unit of consumption at the time for the narrative arc of the album to be an artistic consideration. First, it was distributed as such via official music industry networks. Second, I would argue that the album does take the listener on a journey from start to finish. The presence of strings, for example, on the opening and final tracks (used in different ways) seem to bookend the album.

---

[29] Griffiths is writing about Radiohead's *OK Computer* which was released in 1997. That album is 53 minutes, 45 seconds, around 5 minutes longer than *OPM*.

[30] CDs can normally hold up to 74 minutes of uncompressed stereo digital audio, whereas standard LPs were released with a running time of between 30 and 45 minutes.

[31] Skinner's second album, *A Grand Don't Come for Free* (2004), is much more akin to a 'concept album' in that the album follows one narrative plot: the protagonist loses £1000 and seeks to recover the money. See Slater, 2011.

With the resurgence of vinyl records in recent years, there has been a vinyl re-pressing in 2013 and a vinyl reissue of *OPM* in 2018. A special edition twentieth-anniversary version of the double LP and boxset was released by Locked On records on 23 April 2022, on burnt orange vinyl, as part of National Record Store Day (Welsh, 2022). In other words, the material formats that music is distributed on tell a parallel story of what formats are popular, trends in playback, and everyday listening practices.

The material importance of the album's paratexts can be demonstrated most strongly by its cover: a photographic depiction of Kestrel House in North London (Hans, 2017). The tower-block building was built in 1978 and reno-vated in 1983 as a residential block of flats on Pickard Street (postcode EC1V 8EN). The photograph was taken by German-born British artist Rut Blees Luxemburg in 1995, soon after she had arrived in London,[32] and is taken with an eight-minute exposure. She had been approached to use it for the album cover by the record label, and she agreed after listening to a few tracks of the album. After the success of the album, an EP with remixes was released in the UK in 2003 as a download only, and released on platforms like Napster (the subsequent legal version) and iTunes, giving a sense of how the physicality of albums was starting to yield to the digital download economy. In other words, this was a release that occurred during a pivotal point for the music industry and, as we will see in Section 9, helped encourage the mainstreaming of more diverse forms of British popular music.

6 Everyday Laddism

As we survey the tracks on the album, the middle tracks on *OPM* include more narrative development than the others, supporting a more sustained story-like form within those tracks. While there were overarching themes in tracks like 'Let's Push Things Forward' (Track 3) and 'Turn the Page' (Track 1), they were perhaps more open to interpretation than the more relatively fixed stories in songs like 'Geezers Need Excitement' (Track 6), 'It's Too Late' (Track 7), 'Too Much Brandy (Track 8), 'Don't Mug Yourself' (Track 9), and 'The Irony of it All' (Track 11). This section looks at these stories, as well as how they evoke a notion of the 'everyday' in white male British youth at the time. One reviewer stated: 'Original Pirate Material, to

---

[32] Luxemburg is currently a Reader in Urban Aesthetics and Senior Research Fellow at the Royal College of Art in London. Her institutional website states that she moved to London to attend the London College of Printing to complete her BA in Photography in 1993. She graduated with an MA in Photography from the University of Westminster in 1996. Her first monograph, *London – A Modern Project*, was published in 1997 and was likely where Locked On Records found her work.

put it plainly, is the most vivid evocation of life as a young person in the UK since Blur's *Parklife*, and yes, even The Clash's first album' (*PopMatters*). In other words, this wasn't the first time that the mundane life of the white British working-class persona had been laid out in musical detail. What we find throughout the album are references to pubs (and drinking), drugs, love, and other aspects of the everyday. Many saw Skinner's persona as the protagonist of these stories, espousing a type of laddish white masculinity that almost celebrates (and mocks) their shortcomings and failures – the figure of the anti-aspirational antihero who has become marginalized in part due to societal circumstances.

Section 4 mentioned reference subjects like food, cars, and videogames, which are signifiers of the everyday. The logo of the Streets is a clipper lighter, suggesting tobacco smokers, but more so with the clipper lighter having associations with helping to aid the smoking of cannabis (one can remove the flint stick and use it to poke down the weed in one's joint). There is a banality to the lyrics, perhaps what Michael Billig calls 'banal national-ism' (1995). One review pointed out that 'His 2002 debut, "Original Pirate Material," was a mini-masterpiece full of clubby beats and pubby lyrics about nothing in particular . . . No matter what he was doing, he never let you forget that there was really nothing to do' (Sanneh, 2006, p. E3). Reynolds's review states:

> But if the album succeeds as more than a critical favorite here, it will be because the very English mundane-ness that Mr. Skinner captures might seem exotic to Americans, numbed by hardcore rap's routine imagery of violence, misogyny and materialism. 'It could almost work here like hip-hop works for Brits – as a fantasy,' he said. 'For Americans it could be like: "Who's he? He says geezer all the time! He's got this weird lifestyle."' And that's what could make British rap more powerful ultimately, because American rap today is a TV show – really conserva-tive. (Reynolds, 2002, p. A28)

The 'plainness' of everyday England is also expressed in a 2015 *Fader* cover story where the grime rapper Skepta observed, 'England is so plain, like a burger with nothing on it. That's why it's so real' (quoted in Myers, 2017). To dig into these narratives and stories in more detail, 'Geezers Need Excitement' tells three stories of violence and confrontation. Verse one recounts a 3am post-club encounter in a takeaway shop. Someone is throw-ing chips and another person gets angry and needs to decide whether or not to start a fight ('And forever you're going to regret that, your choice of path'). Verse two discusses Billy, someone who owes their drug dealer money. The dealer, backed up by 'two fat fucks', looks for Billy and his money. Verse three tells of someone who meets a woman ('this bird after pub closing hours') and goes to a club. He thinks about cheating on his girlfriend, but before he can think any longer, he sees his girlfriend kissing another man and he begins to fill with rage and confront the man. In each instance, Skinner as narrator warns the protagonist of the verse to think through their actions, as they will regret it. We travel from the club to the takeaway, traversing spaces of the urban UK city that such archetypes inhabit. It is didactic while painting a stereotypical picture of male youth in the country. The beat of the track echoes the chaos of the night, looped but choppy, phrases seemingly cut off too early.

Skinner dedicates the album in general to 'all the geezers who beat me up or taxed me – you drove me to be so focused' which Ross Diamond (2002) points out in his review of the album:

> This is the story of what is happening to a generation of urban kids growing up knowing they'll be taxed (that's 'mugged', for those readers over 30) of anything of value at least every six months during their school years. It is the sound of a thousand very small and very illegal radio stations, the sound of overheard pub discussion around deals 'for a few dodgy PlayStations', where the only drug to be avoided is the angry alcohol in someone else's bloodstream, where geezers live empty lives of 'football and smut', and where salvation is provided only by those first few, never-to-be-repeated, Ecstasy nights. (Diamond, 2002)

We will see this later on in the nostalgia of the track 'Weak Become Heroes' (covered in more detail in the next section), but the nostalgia for club nights helps to paint a picture of those nights in similar ways to 'Don't Mug Yourself' or 'Geezers Need Excitement' do. In many ways, lyrics in these songs depict a young man moving from adolescence to adulthood, painting it with a social realism that gives an impression of what it is like to be young in an urban environment with little opportunities for social mobility.

Owen Myers (2017), in a review of the album fifteen years after the release, nostalgically reflects on *OPM* and its place in his own youth and considers the 'slice of life' presented to be more nuanced than that of other bands at the time (such as The Libertines):

> At my high school in the London suburbs, it mattered which album you had on your Discman in 2002: the slice-of-life narratives of The Streets's Original Pirate Material . . . Skinner shaded the stories of Englishmen with the nuance they deserved, whether they were puffed-up with pride, or had fallen on hard times with 'a wounded soldier stance.' At a time when U.K. prime minister Tony Blair's introduction of anti-social behaviour orders (ASBOs) in 1998

had further stigmatised lower income families, Original Pirate Material's empathetic narratives of working-class life were a crucial counterpoint. (Myers, 2017)

One example of an expanded narrative is the song 'It's too Late', which refers to being too late to repair a broken relationship. The male protagonist of the song wants to meet his girlfriend/love interest 'at the gates at 8' but he was late as he had to meet a mate. In verse two he tells of how she stood by his side and took it for granted. Verse three is him at the gates and waiting for her, but it was 'too little too late'. He realizes he has failed: 'I purchase a hazy escape at the alcohol place, in the Chase/Sat down, I got a fat frown/Weeping and drowning my senses/For this love game's expensive/I walk in a trance/ Got a wounded soldier stance/The everyday geezers' stares throw me off balance/Now nothing holds significance/and Nothing holds relevance/Cause the only thing I can see is her elegance.' It is a fairly routine story of love lost, like 'Geezers', it is general enough that many people could relate to this story. Interestingly, it is the only time we hear a female voice on the whole album, Jackie Rawe, who sings in unison with Skinner for the chorus:

> I didn't know that it was over
> 'Til it was too late (Too late)
> But if I ever needed you
> Would you be there?

The sadness in track 7 jump cuts to the humour of track 8 in 'Too Much Brandy'. It's another moralizing tale, and this time about someone who has travelled to Amsterdam and has consumed too much drugs and drink: 'We eat junk food, sat drunk on the Tube/Every time the train clunks I feel like puking/Wonder whether that beautiful bird'll ring/Then it all goes hazy.' They end up back at the bar and drink again ('Bad idea to start again late, should've given my brain a break/Take it easy mate, you start to think you're a state, you definite are a state.' The chorus has Skinner perform a childlike, singsong melody which goes, 'In its own little way my body was trying to say that you better stop drinking brandy.' The title, and the chorus kind of gives away the punchline, but as Skinner recounts the evening which gets hazier and hazier, we are not left with a definitive conclusion to the story, only what is alluded to in the refrain. He may have passed out, puked, gone to hospital, but we the listener are left to contemplate the ending for ourselves.

Track 9 ('Don't Mug Yourself') discussed the morning debrief (over a full English breakfast) between a man and his friend Cal who ultimately recommends 'Don't Mug Yourself', as in don't rob/sabotage yourself, but also referencing the British slang phrase 'Don't be a mug' where a mug is someone easily deceived by other people. In other words, Cal warns his friend to not be deceived by this girl, and not to get too involved with her. The music video features a café and full English breakfast followed by the evening drinking pints in a pub, signifiers of the everyday in England.

Track 11 ('The Irony of It All') is an exchange between a man who likes to drink pints of beer vs. someone who enjoys smoking weed. Terry enjoys getting drunk at weekends, spits in the face of an officer yet claims to have never broken the law through his drinking. Tim points out that his weed habit is illegal and 'in the eyes of society I need to be in jail, for the choice of herbs I inhale.' He sees no threat, and there have not been any recorded deaths from marijuana use ('You know I don't see why I should be the criminal/How can something with no recorded fatalities be illegal/And how many deaths are there per year from alcohol'). Terry becomes irate by the third verse, pointing out these 'drugs and criminals, those thugs are the pinnacle of the downfall of society/I've got all the anger pent up inside me'. Verse 4 has a still calm Tim ('we're friendly peaceful people'), discussing how he stays at home smoking, ordering pizza ('We didn't order chicken. Not a problem, we'll pick it out') and playing video games and watching TV. Terry continues to be enraged and starts to repeat himself. When Tim points this out, he gets even more enraged. When Terry tells Tim 'Go get a job and stop robbing us of our taxes', Tim responds, 'Err, well actually according to research, Government funding for further education pales in insignificance when compared to how much they spend on repairing lairy drunk people at the weekend in casualty wards all over the land.' This is the final straw, and Terry threatens to 'batter' him until the song ends abruptly on that note. These two characters signify two manifestations of white British stereotypes of youth in the deprived Britain that Myers had outlined earlier. In this case, a working-class 'geezer' who gets drunk and fights, and a weed smoker who may have too much leisure time due in part to a lack of employment opportunities.

Like the two characters in Eminem's 'Stan' (2000), in 'The Irony of it All', we have a back and forth of two characters played by the same rapper. In response to the false comparisons with Eminem including them being of similar class background, Skinner commented, 'Oh, I suppose it's because we're both white and we both tell stories . . . I'm not as angry as he is, although I don't think he's as angry as he is, either.' While they both speak over the beat in these cases, and neither utilize Black Vernacular English or Multicultural Youth English, Eminem's positionality is close to being within the culture he raps about. But like Eminem, Skinner's songs have been treated as autobiography in many cases of its reception, and the marginality has been around class, part of a collective marginality which links global hip-hop to each other. In other words, hip-hop often most usefully becomes the vehicle to voice artists who are marginal in some way: this might be a marginality around race or ethnicity, gender, or class (Osumare, 2001). While there are many differences between the two artists, Eminem, who reached a high level of global success and recognition only a few years earlier, would help others to process and interpret Skinner's persona, at least for Americans at the start of Skinner's career.

Whiteness as a concept (and masculinity) has been much theorized in American academia in particular (Berger et. al., 1995; Clatterbaugh, 1997; DiPiero, 2002; Kimmel, 2013; Robinson, 2000; Rose, 2014; Smith, 1996; White, 2019; Yancey, 2004). As well as contextualizing a certain form of white working-class masculinity in the British context, Skinner's lyrics and its delivery perform vulnerability, and writers like Jeffrey Boakye have theorized that Skinner has access to vulnerability as a white man in ways that Black grime artists have not. Boakye cites multiple reviews of Skinner's work (NME 2005; BBC 2002; Spin 2001) to show that Mike Skinner's portrayal of mundane white middle-/working-class life made it 'incredibly easy' for the mainstream to accept him as 'the voice of an authentic Britain' (Boakye, 2017, p. 80).

Given the genres that Skinner was working in, it would have been easy for him to be dismissed based on his race. But as Boakye points out, '"Has It Come to This?" makes a virtue of all the things that would detract from Skinner's credibility: his whiteness, his non-Londonness, his lack of polish as a lyricist, his mundane, middle-class-disguised-as-working-class existence, his disinclination towards violence, his introspective musings, his muted braggadocio' (Boakye, 2017, pp. 78–79).

While this persona was successful for Skinner, the tropes of white English masculinity meant that some fans and listeners felt like it wasn't for them. Ruth Saxelby writes, 'I appreciated the wink in his delivery, but they weren't made for me: they were geared towards a generation of young men battling within the rigid limitations of masculinity' (quoted in Myers, 2017). She goes onto lament the fact that as his career progressed, she felt somewhat abandoned as a female listener.

Boakye writes that 'He was a safe option, telling a story that the mainstream was ready and willing to believe in. It wouldn't be until 2003 that the mainstream would be ready, or at least invited, to accept the loud desperation of Black adolescence via Dizzee Rascal's equally acclaimed debut, *Boy in da Corner*' (Boakye, 2017, p. 81).[33] In the long history of white artists becoming more commercially successful in mainstream popular music, Boakye argues

---

[33] It is worth mentioning that Rascal's single 'I Luv U' came out in 2002 as with many other early grime singles, so it would be fictitious to suggest that Skinner's *OPM* leads to the creation of grime, but, as I argue later, many have agency in helping to mainstream it.

that Skinner's white persona maintains a status quo that at least white listeners could relate to more than the difference performed by artists (and genres) coded as ethnic minority.

Skinner's success helps expand the doors for grime to thrive in the mainstream (see Section 9), but given his whiteness, he was able to flip 'every expectation of urban masculinity just before Grime would define the rules of urban masculinity for the next 15 years' (Boakye, 2017, p. 79). Boakye uses the short career of the Mitchell Brothers, a Black grime group who also focused in on vulnerability, and were signed to Skinner's record label, to argue that 'black vulnerability just doesn't have the same legs as its white counterpart' (Boakye, 2017, p. 83).[34] The social realism of The Streets could be compared with the kitchen sink dramas of the 1960s or films like *Saturday Night and Sunday Morning* which offer a depiction of the post-WWII white working class in England. And, of course, any perceived marginality of class is still within white norms, society as dominated by those racialized as white, subject to the white gaze. Whiteness is not 'Other', even while white Englishness may have been exoticized by American listeners, it is still part of the dominant system. They are beneficiaries of the system, even if not signatories to it.

The final song on *OPM* is 'Stay Positive', a powerful track which urges the listener to stay positive, especially if they are going through a tough time. The song centres on addiction, moving from weed consumption to heroin: 'Weed becomes a chore/ You want the buzz back, so you follow the others onto smack.' He opens the second verse with, 'Feels nice and still/ Good thing about brown [heroin] is it always will/ It's easy, no-one blames you/ It's that world out there that's fucked you/ You're no less of a person and if God exists, He still loves you/ Just remember that'. Skinner himself says that the post-industrial landscape of Birmingham, and people without work turning to drugs was an inspiration for the song. In his autobiography, he described with reference to this song that many people in Birmingham had moved from weed to heroin, but is also at pains to state that despite misconceptions, 'Stay Positive' is not about his own drug struggle – his voice was creaky because he 'just happened to have a cold at the time' (Skinner, 2012, p. 59).[35] His voice-with-cold provides an additional element to the vulnerable quality of his persona, and more so than even his other

---

[34] The Ghanaian-British rap duo were also the first signing from Mike Skinner's record label The Beats.

[35] Skinner wrote 'Stay Positive' in the flat in Darlinghurst next to King's Cross in Sydney. Skinner writes, 'The funny thing about 'Stay Positive' is, you can't really hear Australia in it. If anything, being away for a year had given me a deeper understanding of what being British meant. Maybe it's easier to make sense of your own experiences once you've seen them from an outside perspective, or had a different situation to compare them with. Because you could say that the

songs. Jon Caramanica commented that the beat included 'a spooked Wu-Tang-style piano' (Caramanica, 2003). He reminds the listener to take care of oneself first, and that when you feel better, do not forget the rock bottom moments:

> But remember that one day, shit might just start crumbling
> Your bird might fuck off or you might lose your job
> It's when that happens that what I'm talking about will feel much more
>   important to you
> So if you ain't feeling it, just be thankful that things are cool in your world

The chorus, Skinner singing 'Just try and stay positive' repeats over and over, and starts to skip and repeat like a skipping record, and the album ends abruptly as what almost sounds like a glitch. This draws one's attention to the idea of the track as a loop at the moment it starts to 'fail'. The album ends sonically where we began, with a string motif and a skipping record. The song was further solidified as depicting bleak urban life with its use in the UK film *Kidulthood* (2006) about urban youths growing up in London.

Skinner's song is open enough that a wide variety of people can relate to it in different ways. One doesn't have to be a heroin addict to appreciate using drugs or alcohol to escape the mundanity of life. Claire Maguire writes, 'His lyrics spoke to me and my friends at the time, when we were 15 or 16. Our nightlife was around places like [chain pub] Wetherspoons. Every Friday night was the same, every day was the same' (Myers, 2017). Skinner himself writes, 'I've met many people since "Stay Positive" came out who've told me that it's meant a lot to them at difficult times in their lives. They're generally people who've been either victims of stabbing or, more often, addicted to heroin' (Skinner, 2012, p. 74).

Klosterman is quick to point out in his album review that 'Skinner has been portrayed as a representative of the working class, a backstreets kid from Birmingham. Skinner, who now lives in London, resists the working-class designation, and insisted his life has been relatively easy' (Klosterman, 2003, p. M24). But, as Boakye notes of the fidelity to Skinner's 'real' life, this doesn't matter since the persona is identifiable: people can identify with it or at least see it in existence in their society. Rap music has been similar, with media and fan reception of gangsta rappers perceived as the bards of life on the streets (including drugs and gangs). This is not to say it is all entirely fiction, but audiences are quick to either identify with confessional rappers

---

subject matter of the song is the state of mind that made me want to leave the country in the first place' (Skinner, 2012, pp. 73–74).

like Eminem that go deep into their own psychology and family challenges, or believe the stories of deviance from gangsta rappers.

Skinner does not believe that songwriters need to live the life they write about. Despite being heavily influenced by his surroundings and his own life, Skinner sees himself as a craftsman more than anything else. He writes,

> People love to ascribe meaning to tiny snippets of information. I do it as much as anyone – not just in life, in songwriting as well. You have to get in and out in three and a half minutes, and that's not enough time to fully encompass how complicated life really is. It's much easier to give people a simple hook to hang an explanation on. (Skinner, 2012, p. 67)

Through many of his songs, Skinner has given us a glimpse of English life, the lives of his characters rather than pure autobiography. Looking at US rap in this way, as craft and storytelling, might enlighten some of the facades and fictions within its milieu as well.

7 Genre: UK Garage and US Hip-Hop

The opening track of *Original Pirate Material* ('Turn the Page') sounds like the commencement of a symphony, albeit a twenty-first-century one, whose digitally produced strings repeat as if on a skipping record, complete with faint vinyl-esque hiss, in anticipation for a beat to drop. Like the atomic opening of Beethoven's 9th symphony (1824), we are waiting for something big to happen. After four bars of strings the beat enters, the kind of broken, glitchy beat one might hear on a UK garage (UKG) track. More strings enter, and after what feels like a long anticipatory intro, my US-based ears hear something many listeners at the time would not necessarily expect: rapping.

Garage music had MCs prior to the moment *OPM* was released in 2002, but no garage MCs sounded like this, and none told stories like these. According to Skinner, the strings took inspiration from the film *Gladiator* (2000), and the lyrics match thematically ('I'm 45th generation Roman', 'soldiers slaying, looks like geezers raving', 'And then the crowds roar', 'Slay warriors in the forests', 'In the afterlife gladiators meet their maker').

By opening the album with strings reminiscent of both Romantic-era symphonies and mainstream Hollywood film music, Skinner musically advises the listener to 'strap in' and be prepared to listen closely. This is echoed lyrically when he says, 'Return to your sittin position and listen.' After this nod to 'epic' symphonic film music, the track rises in intensity which pulls the listener into the drama, and the album transitions abruptly to its first single, 'Has it come to this?' It has the feel of a D-I-Y track for pirate radio, accompanied with DJ-like talk over ('Original pirate material, lock down your aerial'). The garage beat has sonic tinges of Artful Dodger and So Solid Crew, but Skinner takes the sounds in a very different direction.

One of the key characteristics of *OPM* is its linking of genres, and two genres in particular: UK garage and US hip-hop. As stated earlier, positive reception of the album often hinged on previous knowledge of UK garage and its emerging popularity as a frame, which peaked around 1999–2001, as well as the tropes of street knowledge, insults, bragging, and wordplay from mainstream US hip-hop of the mid-to-late 1990s. Skinner added his own local nuance and accent to his stories, and we have seen influences from punk, ska, reggae, and other dance genres like house. In Skinner's own words, he discusses his inability to work in one genre only:

> I've never been able to make a genre record. It seems it's impossible for me to come up with music that is convincingly part of a scene. I've really tried, but whether it was rap, house or garage, it always seemed like there was something inside me that was too playful to stay within the guidelines. I can't not make stuff that's a bit . . . *outside*. (Skinner, 2012, p. 80)

But of all the genres that he draws from, this section discusses the two primary genre-based influences on *OPM*: UK garage and US hip-hop.[36] The history of UK garage and US hip-hop, and their convergence, tells a complicated tale of multicultures and migration, as well as influence and innovation in the underground. In both cases, it was about creating something new which excited dancers/partygoers/clubbers/ravers, and eventually was absorbed into the mainstream of the music industry, mutating (or whitewashed, as some might say) into a commercially successful recorded commodity. Audiences frustrated with the mainstream flattening out of more underground popular music styles, and with artists who would become too far removed from the streets, would then move on to the next new thing, which in this case in the UK would become other styles such as dubstep and grime.

To start with a discussion of garage music as the first half of the *OPM* hybrid, the UK variant of the genre emerges in early 1990s London. The rave culture that Reynolds discusses in *Energy Flash* as the Second Summer of Love (1988) had gone from free outdoor parties and illegal underground warehouses to (legal) mainstream clubs in the early 1990s. It had received a bad reputation as an underground phenomenon because of drugs like ecstasy. A moral panic was created by negative media coverage, and as a result, the raves had changed

---

[36] Important studies on genre include Negus (1999), Holt (2007), and Kronengold (2022). Two books that deal excellently with racialized categories of genre in the US music industry are Miller (2010) and Brackett (2016).

their reputation and more mainstream clubs emerged such as Ministry of Sound (founded in 1991). Breakbeat hardcore would fragment into a number of genres by 1992–1993, including UK garage. Certain DJs at the time were becoming particularly influenced by American DJs such as Todd Edwards and the developments happening at the discotheque Paradise Garage in New York City. Titmus writes:

> An ode to New York City, Ministry [of Sound] attempted to import the glamour and grit of The Paradise Garage to a grey area of South London famous for little other than a massive roundabout. The club had even gone to the huge effort of buying an identical sound rig to The Garage and had convinced New Jersey house godfather, Tony Humphries, to take a residency. It was an aspirational and American experience quite unlike anything UK clubbers were used to. (Titmus, 2019)

US garage as a style was named after Paradise Garage, as garage was originally the term used for house music in NYC, as opposed to Chicago house which was initially known as deep house. Early examples include Taana Gardiner's 'Heartbeat' (1981), Peech Boys's 'Don't Make me Wait' (1982) and Visual's 'The Music Got Me' (1983). It was perceived in the UK as more soulful compared to genres like jungle by the mid 1990s (New York garage tended to have gospel-like vocals) and would often be included in a second room on jungle nights in clubs. In other words, these clubs were looking to the US for initial influence before it transformed into something of their own.

US garage inspired UK house and breakbeat DJs to add their own UK spin on the style, often considered darker, dirtier, rougher around the edges (Titmus, 2019). This coincided with a desire for after-parties on Sunday after raves at clubs like Ministry of Sound. DJs and partygoers would find themselves across the road at a Pub called The Elephant and Castle (in eponymous area of London) on Sunday morning and continuing into the afternoon. This became known as the 'Sunday Scene'.[37] Happy Days (launched by Timi Ram Jam) became the name of the club night which splintered off from AWOL (A Way of Life) at Ministry of Sound,[38] which aimed to catch the clubbers after the Ministry of Sound closed. Resident DJs at Happy Days (Matt Jam, Mickey Simms, and Justin Cantor) played house music at a faster tempo. Given the fact that clubbers had been going all night at 120 bpm, the after-party music needed to be faster to keep them going, with UK garage at around 130 bpm (Titmus, 2019).

---

[37] Titmus, 'Nightclubbing'

[38] Other venues of note at the time are Turnmills (opened in 1990), Heaven, and Camden Palace, the latter two of which had been nightclubs in the 1980s, but played a prominent role in the UK dance music scene of the 1990s. My thanks to Marko Higgins for pointing out these important venues to me.

This new style of music would become known as speed garage due to the faster tempos compared to its American cousin, and its kick drum pattern.[39] Prominent examples include 'Sugar Is Sweeter (Armand's Drum 'n' Bass Mix)' (1996), Double 99's 'RipGroove' (1997), and Groove Armada's 'Superstylin'' (2001). It spread to other venues in London. In 1994 there was Happy Sundays at the Arches behind Charing Cross towards Embankment, The Park in Kennington, Café de Paris and the Gass Club in Leicester Square. The support from the pirate radio stations by entities such as Rinse FM, Girls FM, London Underground, Ice FM, Flex FM and Déjà vu helped UK garage break through to the mainstream toward the late 1990s (de Lacey, 2019).

UK garage was a largely underground movement in the early-to-mid 1990s, multicultural, largely working class, and initially London based. In addition to the faster tempos, UK garage had a larger use of bass frequencies and is linked to UK bass culture (dub, reggae, jungle/drum & bass, grime, dubstep; Bradley, 2001). Likeminded DJs such as Norris 'Da Boss' Windross, Daryl B, Dominic 'Spreadlove' and Hermit were pioneers of UK garage and would play the important venues interchangeably. Lexis and Dr. Love (2014) describe that by the mid-1990s, Happy Days had moved from Elephant and Castle, to the Frog and Nightgown and then to The Arches, a warehouse which held up to 1000 people. In Lexis and Dr. Love's history of the genre (2014), 1995 is seen as a high point for UK garage, gaining lots of steam but not yet fully into the mainstream. UK garage thrived in 'superclubs' in the late 1990s and early 2000s, which often blurred this distinction between underground and mainstream, and was a very multicultural mix of participants, owners, and artists (Lexis and Dr. Love, 2014).

The genre would continue to change and create stylistic offshoots which are still debated in terms of their categorizations. R&B vocals were added to beats and an offshoot called 2-step garage became particularly popular.[40] Some of the more notable 2-step garage tracks include 'Sweet Like Chocolate' (1999) by Shanks & Bigfoot which reached number 1 on the singles chart in May 1999, and 'Re-Rewind' by Craig David and the Artful Dodger which reached number 2 by the end of November 1999. These two songs, alongside 'With a Little Bit of Luck' (by DJ Luck and MC Neat, released Dec 1999) were heavily playlisted on UK radio at the end of the millennium.

---

[39] Though more complicated than space will allow here, speed garage is now considered a subgenre of UK garage, with sped-up NY garage 4 to the floor rhythms combined with breakbeats.

[40] There is debate within fan communities and message boards over whether the 2-step beat is just that, a beat pattern which is used in UK garage, or an entire genre called '2-step'. For our purposes, it is the 2-step beats of garage which added vocals and became popular in the mainstream.

In 2001, the UK garage music group DJ Pied Piper and the Masters of Ceremonies released 'Do You Really Like it' (released in May, reaching number 1), So Solid Crew's '21 Seconds' reached number 1 in August of the same year, and the debut single of Daniel Bedingfield, 'Gotta Get Thru This', was released in November 2001 and went to number one on the UK singles chart in 2001 and 2002. So Solid Crew and their success are a very important part to this story, not least that '21 Seconds' is considered to bridge the gap between 2-step garage and what would eventually become grime (the track is often considered to be 'proto-grime'). The song, and its music video, features each member of the collective rapping for twenty-one seconds. It was also important for racial representation, as many grime artists have pointed to the '21 Seconds' video as one of the first times they saw someone from London who looked like them in a music video. Many have also pointed to their televised performance at the BRIT awards that year as an important moment for diversity and representation in the UK mainstream. In addition to their iconic performance, So Solid Crew won the BRIT award that year for best British Video of the Year. 2-step also helped to solidify UK garage as its own genre specific to the UK, also reflecting the broken beats heard at the time in hardcore and jungle. The asymmetry left it open especially in the low end for bigger bass lines in the genre.[41]

The mainstream success of So Solid Crew predates *OPM*, and was an important context for the success of that album. Other acts with mainstream success (Craig David, The Artful Dodger, Daniel Bedingfield) signalled that garage's underground status was now well and truly over. Skinner's success, as well as So Solid Crew's success, would also help facilitate the mainstreaming of urban music genres such as grime, as we will discuss in Section 9. Dan Hancox writes in *Inner City Pressure*:

> In the first two years of the millennium, UK garage was being stretched in two directions at once – a process which is always likely to make something break in the middle. On the one hand, the poppy, commercial end was thriving, and producing numerous hits: singer-MCs like Craig David, Ms Dynamite and Daniel Bedingfield became stars, and tunes like Sweet Female Attitude's 'Flowers' and DJ Luck and MC Neat's 'With A Little Bit Of Luck' were ubiquitous. But something was pulling hard in the opposite musical direction – to the dark side. On this side of UK garage's personality split, mostly male MCs dominated instead of crooning singers; the instrumentals conjured not a glitzy VIP area but a low-lit council estate … When catchy, sample-heavy novelty records like DeeKline's 'I Don't Smoke' started to take off in the garage clubs, and the likes of Heartless Crew, So Solid Crew and Pay As U Go Cartel started to have hits themselves, the divisions deepened. (Hancox, 2018, p. 48)

---

[41] My thanks to Ivan Mouraviev for bringing up this important point. He also notes that the '4 on the floor' beat patterns were much more associated with the US house sound.

In addition to garage, it is also worth noting the influence of the French house music duo Daft Punk on Skinner as well. He enjoyed their idea of a musical persona separate from any semblance of personal identity in performance, as Daft Punk would perform in helmets to try and create a sense of anonymity. He was very influenced by the *Homework* album (Skinner, 2012, p. 54), and has stated that the shout out to people in 'Who Got the Funk?' was influenced by a Daft Punk track which does a similar act of naming, and can be found in plenty of hip-hop songs as well (for example, The Roots's, 'WAOK (Ay) Rollcall' (2002); Rodan 'Roll Call' (2004)).

Turning back to hip-hop influences, Skinner writes:

> The thing about hip-hop artists in the nineties that influenced me the most, apart from their music, was the fact that you never saw them. People like Redman or Mobb Deep or Inspectah Deck from Wu-Tang Clan didn't seem to do interviews, appear on Top of the Pops, or come to England in any capacity whatsoever. The mystique became very deeply engrained in my idea of how people who made music should conduct themselves. (Skinner, 2012, pp. 11–12)

Skinner had assumed that because the hip-hop artists didn't go to the UK they were reclusive as well (Skinner 2012, p. 12).

Track 12 on *OPM* is called 'Weak Become Heroes' and is about the nostalgia of clubbing. Skinner admits in his autobiography (p. 30) that his UK garage knowledge came from listening at home and in the car, but he has also discussed going to clubs however infrequently (Skinner, 2012, p. 51). 'Tune reminds me of my first E', most likely a reference to the club drug ecstasy. He goes on to rap 'Unique, still 16 and feeling horny, point the sky and feel free/See here people are all equal'. In the second verse The Streets remembers 'chatting to this bloke in the toilets/ Dizzy new hights blinded by the lights[42]/ these people are for life'. By the final verse, Skinner raps, 'Then the girl in the café taps me on the shoulder/I realize 5 years went by and I'm older/Memories moulder, winter's colder/But that same piano loops over and over and over.' The character has been in a café all along, aged 21, hearing a song over the speakers that reminds him of five years ago and going to raves. The accompanying track is a looped beat perhaps more reminiscent of US house music than UK garage. There is a looped piano riff, and in the chorus Skinner sings:

> We were just standing there, minding our own
> We went on and on (We all smile, we all sing)
> The weak become heroes and the stars align
> (We all sing, we all sing, think)

---

[42] 'Blinded by the Lights' was the name of the third single from his second album *A Grand Don't Come for Free* (2004) and is another track about partying with the music video depicting him having too much to drink and taking drugs at a wedding, ending in a fight with fellow guests.

What Saxelby calls one of his 'rave ballads' (quoted in Myers, 2017) the song could refer to any experience with rave or club culture. It is painted as a utopian space – people who are normally considered weak can be heroes. The notion of time passing is glossed over ('hours fly over') and the club becomes a place to 'discover new worlds'. In it we see the conviviality of Paul Gilroy's multicultural London. The music video for the track (which was the third single released from the album) depicts this: Skinner in the café looking back to the times he was in the club. He addresses the camera, leading the audience into his nostalgic experiences. It is something many could relate to, the nostalgia for an earlier time in your youth. It is an aspect of the everyday, but spans both the day in the café and nights in the club so we get a fuller picture of 'a day in the life' of Britain's youth. Sonically, the beat itself feels like a US house / garage piano riff, with an overdriven square wave bass timbre (from dancehall – hardcore -jungle and UKG).

The song's final lines are also worth some mention: 'Out of respect of Johnny Walker,[43] Paul Oakenfold, Nicky Holloway, Danny Rampling and all the people who gave us these times/And to the government, I stick my middle finger up with regard to the Criminal Justice Bill.' After mentioning the important DJs associated with pioneering raves in the UK, he cites the Criminal Justice and Public Order act of 1994. Introduced by Michael Howard, Home Secretary under the John Major Conservative government (1990–1997), this act changed the law to restrict and reduce existing rights, clamped down on unlicensed rave parties, and gave greater penalties for certain 'anti-social' behaviours.[44] A social policy like this one potentially adds to the nostalgia of a time when raves were more ubiquitous and their questionable legality added to the romance of the scene.

Turning to hip-hop as the other half of the influence equation, like 1990s London, the 1970s Bronx, NYC, was also a breeding ground for combining elements and influences from multicultural youth cultures who wanted to party. Kool Herc came from Jamaica, played funk and Latin breakbeats with his Jamaican inspired soundsystem, to a mostly African American and Latino audience in the 1970s South Bronx. DJ Afrika Bambaataa would expand the variety of breakbeats from Kraftwerk to The Monkees, and Grandmaster Flash would make it a show to be viewed as a virtuosity display of turntable skills

---

[43] These four DJs are mythologized as those who went to Ibiza in August 1987, went to club Amnesia, and brought back a missionary zeal for what would become known as rave (see Warren, 2007).

[44] https://publications.parliament.uk/pa/cm200203/cmbills/008/03008.i-viii.html.

(Chang, 2004). Again drawn from Jamaican soundsystem culture, MCs would hype up the DJ-led parties, and vocal rapping increased in prominence as the practices moved to commercial recordings from 1979 onwards.

Hip-Hop is increasingly popularized in the mid-1980s with the rise of digital sampling technologies, national tours, and dedicated rap labels such as Def Jam. While this golden age is said to end with major labels taking over and promoting gangsta rap in the mainstream (around 1993 with the success of Dr. Dre's *The Chronic*; Chang, 2004), hip-hop in the 1990s was a varied affair if one looked underground and in pockets other than the mainstream singles chart (Watkins, 2005). Rappers such as Nas and collectives such as the Wu Tang Clan were huge influences on Skinner. Skinner has said his favourite rappers are RZA followed by Raekwon, Rakim and Nas's album *Illmatic*. Skinner writes, 'I still love *Illmatic*, but 'Triumph' on *Wu-Tang Forever* is one of the anthems of my life. In that respect, it's up there with 'Burnin'' by Daft Punk' (Skinner, 2012, pp. 24–25).

Skinner was first exposed to hip-hop through the Beastie Boys's album *License to Ill*. Following this, he writes that 'The first album I ever owned for myself was Vanilla Ice's *II The Extreme,* which I got for Christmas when I was eleven' (Skinner, 2012, p. 39). 'Hip-Hop as I experienced it was very much an indoor thing. I was born a bit too late for boom-boxes and break-dance mats. I remember my brother doing The Caterpillar in the living room and me having a go as well' (Skinner, 2012, p. 42). He was making loops of Run DMC song bits and pause button tapes in his bedroom, as many hip-hop fans were doing in the 1980s and 1990s, and received his first set of turntables when he was sixteen years old (Skinner, 2012, pp. 35–36).

Skinner had thought of garage MCs as a specifically British form of rapper. He felt, however, that the rapping wasn't 'up to much' at first (Skinner, 2012, p. 25). He notes that 'Rap music was not seen as accessible because it was inherently American. It was what everyone really wanted to be doing, but there was no hope of breaking through and getting any attention once you'd admitted that' (Skinner, 2012, p. 26). He felt garage MCs had career possibilities but none of the status, and like the early days of hip-hop, where they were primarily to get people on the dance floor and more aligned with Jamaican MC traditions like toasting.

In terms of hip-hop's popularity in the UK, especially with home-grown hip-hop groups, it was very underground in the 1990s. And in the early days of speed-garage (like early UK hip-hop), a lot of MCs were putting on American accents. After garage became more popular, the accents became more British. Being based in Birmingham, Skinner had to contend with the two biggest genres there in heavy rock and reggae. Furthermore, according to Skinner's autobiography, labels initially didn't know what to do with his tracks. American rap labels for example wondered why they would hire an Englishman making Wu Tang–style rap when they have plenty of rappers in that style over there in New York City, and his house music didn't quite fit in the mould of house either:

> At that point, making house music was probably where my professional future lay – insofar as I had one – but the stuff I did was always a bit weird. I'd be sending it to London labels and they'd say 'This isn't house music, it's got a sampled orchestra on it.' Nothing I did quite seemed to fall into step . . . . And was trying too hard to make hip-hop tracks in an East Coast (Wu-Tang) style. (Skinner, 2012, p. 55)

Before garage came along, UK youth seemed to have to make a choice between their preference for house music or rap music. Skinner liked both of course. He writes:

> Before garage came along, it was always a choice between rap or house, and for me the answer was 'both'. By that time I'd already got into making hip-hop. I knew loads of rappers who lived near me, and I used to make beats for them. But when I got the turntables, that was more about house music. All the rappers who used to come round my house and smoke weed in my bedroom called me 'House-boy'. (Skinner, 2012, p. 50)

Skinner also notes that in America, there are homophobic associations with disco (and electronic dance music traditions) and he sees the shift to a more heteronormative and hypermasculine form for rap in America because of this, but that prejudice did not exist in England because there was the template of the acid house rave, and so electronic dance music and other R&B forms could coexist a little more easily in places.

Marko Higgins's work on UK dubstep (forthcoming) looks at the origins and evolution of the genre (and its subsequent mainstreaming in the US) as a convergence (in the Henry Jenkins sense) of jungle and garage music. A similar convergence happens with The Streets but with UK garage and East Coast US hip-hop. Multiple genres occupy different rooms of the same venue, such as at Fabric and Ministry of Sound. Higgins discusses genre fusion and development within an evolutionary framework, and such a method seems especially fertile for the study of electronic dance music-based cultures.

The tenth track on the album, called 'Who Got the Funk?' is a funky instrumental track featuring a wah-wah sounding guitar and horns. It is an opportunity for Skinner to shout out cities, the record label, and various individuals who have helped Skinner or contributed to the album: Lee

Satchell (Calvin's brother, mentioned in 'Don't Mug Yourself', and sung by Calvin Bailey),[45] Crispy,[46] Rosco, England's Glory, Uniq, Locked On, Andy Lewis, Birmingham, London, Barnet, Brixton, Beckenham. The lyrics state 'this is just a groove' as if to make a distinction perhaps with the more song-like tracks on the album. It provides both sonic variety and a slightly different pace at under two minutes (1:53), as a transitional track or interval.

The penultimate track on the album sonically resembles the work of the Wu Tang Clan more than others in terms of its beat, but its lyrics discuss Skinner's origins 'raised as a Northern star with a London underground travelcard' and brags of having the latest Nikes. 'Lock on to 102.6 The Streets' – it returns the listener to the start of the album, a freestyle-sounding delivery which confidently raps about both Skinner's prowess as an artist while celebrating the everyday ('street geezers, accept me as your own'), mentioning Kronenburg and 'double doves' (ecstasy) and 'herbs' (marijuana). It's a short track, essentially one verse long, and transitions into the final track on the album, 'Stay Positive', which perhaps ironically talks about the difficulties of getting over addictions.

This rap and garage combination, as we have seen, is crucial to The Streets and its creation, which Skinner explains best in his own words:

> Even though I designed it to be something quite slick in some ways, the basic vision behind The Streets was very simple: people really like garage, but no one's really saying anything worth listening to on the records – it's just a load of words; American rappers are saying stuff that people care about, and everyone listens to them. So my plan was to say stuff that people cared about, but over garage beats. Although I saw myself mainly as a producer, I'd been rapping more and more because I didn't really trust anyone else to tell the kind of stories I wanted to hear. (Skinner, 2012, p. 30)

In this sense, the garage MCs Skinner refers to (including a track like '21 Seconds') could be interpreted as part of the Afrodiasporic traditions of Signifyin(g), where the signifier is foregrounded over the signified. Tracks like 'Let's Push Things Forward' or 'Sharp Darts' are more in that tradition than the more narrative story-based tracks discussed in Section 6. As we will see next, a lot of material on the album could be considered the result of convergences that bring together multiple worlds: not only convergences of genre, but of the local and the global, to the Afrodiasporic and Eurocentric, to create a unique work greater than the sum of its parts.

---

[45] Calvin Bailey is Skinner's friend and provided the vocals on 'Don't Mug Yourself'.
[46] Crispy is frontman of Mouth Almighty and had accused Skinner of stealing his material for some of *OPM*.

PART III: ORIGINAL

8 Little England Meets Big England: Hybridity as Originality

As the last section has shown, the formula of combining approaches from US hip-hop music and UK garage was a key ingredient to the construction of *OPM* and no doubt helped to contribute to its success. This combination of genres, alongside the other stylistic influences and Skinner's own localism and accent, gave it an original feel. The *Original* and *Pirate* in the title suggest a deliberate oxymoronic play on words, and I would like to extend that paradoxical spirit to posit the following: the album's originality does not lie in the uniqueness of musical material or subject matter, but it is the particular *combination* of elements that makes this album an original product of its time.

A pure unadulterated notion of originality in any form of art, not least music, is a myth. It is a myth, however, that has been used by modernists and postmodernists alike. As discussed in Section 4, Skinner understands nothing is original, as alluded to by his album title *Everything Is Borrowed*. And yet, how originality is *performed* or not in intertextual works is a crucial component that has been discussed for, say, musical borrowing in hip-hop music (Williams, 2013). In the case of *OPM*, the convergences of previous material give rise to new sounds (especially as interpreted by American audiences who may have grown up with different musical traditions). Rather than fetishize what is 'new' here, I want to create an opportunity to explore the album as a unique convergence of factors.

To do this, I would like to revisit the everyday localism of 'Little England' and the idea of the hyperlocal in the stories that Skinner tells,[47] in combination with the 'Big England' of Section 2, in order to think about the postcolonial hybridities involved in *OPM*. Both little England and big England need to be embraced to understand the multi-layered contexts of the album.

Despite the triple-city (London, Birmingham, Sydney) sites of production, English localism is strongly represented lyrically, musically, and visually. Many of the themes and ideas represent what we might consider signifiers of Englishness: drinking tea, supporting football, going to the pub, or eating takeaways. Music videos for 'Don't Mug Yourself', 'The Irony of It All', and 'Weak Become Heroes' paint a picture of the local, of little England and a 'slice of life' perspective that as Partridge (2015) notes can be found in California gangsta rap or golden era New York City rap videos. The 'banal nationalism' (Billig, 1995) of certain signifiers of Englishness – football, tea, fish and chips, English breakfast – is an everyday representation of the nation

---

[47] For an excellent case study of the hyperlocal, focusing on the Newham area of London, see White (2020).

that builds a sense of national belonging. Billig (1995) considers this in contrast with forms of 'hot nationalism' that are the more flag-waving variety: seen at international sporting events, royal occasions, and citizenship ceremonies.

The nostalgia that Skinner feels in 'Weak Become Heroes' is an urban one, a slight variation on the postcolonial melancholia that in this instance doesn't point to WWII as the site of nostalgia, but instead draws from late 1980s/early 1990s rave culture instead. Furthermore, his portrayal of the white working-class urban youth figure has solidified and further popularized an archetype which Tyler (2012) discusses was floating around at the time. From the British television world, for example, the top three most viewed television programmes in 2002 were *Only Fools and Horses* (16.3 million), *EastEnders* (16 million), and *Coronation Street* (15 million), all depictions of (largely) white working-class life in Britain.

One of the stereotypes within this milieu, which admittedly Skinner borrowed from and contributed to, would be the figure of the 'chav'. This term was added to the *Oxford English Dictionary* in 2004 and is defined by them as 'an offensive word for somebody, usually a young person, who you think behaves, dresses or speaks in a way that shows their low social class and lack of education'. The stereotype was in the popular consciousness one year after *OPM* on the sketch comedy show *Little Britain* (2003–2007). The character Vicky Pollard, a tracksuit–wearing 'chav' played by Matt Lucas, was a stereotype who over-consumed beyond her means, was moody, loud, untrustworthy, smokes cigarettes, had a strong Bristolian accent, and had her hair tied tight into a 'Croydon facelift'. By series 3 she was depicted as having twelve children, and tried to claim money with a fake lottery ticket. The Pollard character contributed to a demonization of the working class which was already a prominent feature in the media (Blacker, 2006; Jones, 2016; Lockyer, 2010; Tyler, 2008). Critics of the show, such as journalist Johann Hari, noted the show a was 'a vehicle for two rich kids [creators Matt Lucas and David Walliams] to make themselves into multimillionaires by mocking the weakest people in Britain [the poor, disabled, elderly, gay, and fat]' (Hari, 2005). A YouGov poll revealed that 70 per cent of those who participated thought that the Vicky Pollard character was an accurate representation of youth in Britain (Lockyer, 2010, p. 126). British sitcoms had been using class as an important storyline for decades, and more recent reality shows, dubbed by Lockyer 'poverty porn' (2010, p. 126), were also depicting British poverty in particular ways for mainstream audiences.

In 2004, Skinner said he was going to feature in *Chav: The Movie*, a celebration of the demographic (Roberts, 2004). In 2008, when he performed at the BBC Electric Proms, he described the performance to be akin to a 'chav wedding' ('Streets To Chav Up Proms', 2008). One journalist described Skinner as 'ex-pat Brummie' and 'self-styled King of the Chavs' with 'Jimmy Savile-like jewellery and council state attire' (Connor, 2005). In short, Skinner played up to the stereotype, capturing and contributing to a particular Zeitgeist in terms of targeting the white underclass of Britain. The chav is racialized as white, becomes Othered alongside immigrants to become scapegoats for wider problems with society (Jones, 2016).

The perceived realism of the album was a feature of many of the reviews of the album: 'This masterpiece of a debut is an assured recovery from Britpop's hangover; a comedown from the euphoria of Cool Britannia and New Labour; and an assured extension of Pulp's Common People with enhanced in-depth realism.'[48] *OPM* was released a year after New Labour's second term election win. As this review suggests, it was not a patriotic celebration of Britishness, but perhaps in part because of the 1997 devolution of some powers to Scotland, Wales, and Northern Ireland, the localism of English identity needed to be explored in more detail in the cultural sphere.

The term 'hybridity' has several connotations, and the way I have used it here could come across as more positive and optimistic than some might believe. I use the term as a greater-than-the-sum-of-its-parts melting pot arena of multiculturalism, perhaps more similar to Samuel Floyd's idea of syncretization (Floyd, 1995) rather than Homi Bhabha's conception of hybridity (Bhabha, 1994).[49] Thinking about the postcolonial roots of some of these signifiers of banal nationalism complicates the notion of Englishness as a straightforward 'local', or even national, affair. Fish and chips, often seen as the traditional English dish, comes from fried fish from Jewish culture and potatoes from Ireland (Alibhai-Brown, 2015), Indian food as a hybrid of British and Indian ingredients, and perhaps most famously Stuart Hall's comments about not a single tea plantation existing in the UK, demonstrate that people like Jamaican-born Hall have been in England and exploited by the nation for centuries (Hall, 1991). In other words, a search for Englishness has revealed that English culture has always been founded on a colonial extraction from perceived 'Others'.

---

[48] Bonnie Cochrane, 'Weak Become Heroes: Original Pirate Material by The Streets Classic Album Review', Soundandvision.blog. 20 April 2020. https://soundandvision.blog/2020/04/20/classic-album-review-original-pirate-material-by-the-streets/.

[49] Goldschmitt defines hybridity as 'A concept for describing musical mixtures that are explicitly enmeshed in identity politics, most often involving racial and ethnic identity, and its effects on culture. As a concept, scholars and critics began using hybridity in music during the late 1980s and early 1990s as postcolonial and critical race theory expanded in influence in North American music scholarship. Previously, "hybrid" referred to mixture involving genre or form'. K. E. Goldschmitt, 'Hybridity'.

Original Pirate Material is a product of this tradition, at once postcolonial given the wide diversity of musical factors and influence, and highly local. While it doesn't fully rectify the 'white amnesia' of the colonial past, it moves closer to a hybrid that fully encompasses both the multicultural local and global.

Skinner is working in a framework of urban multiculturalism which allows him to navigate a number of influences at once (James, 2015). There is also another perspective one could take: that of cultural appropriation, or of the white appropriation of Black music, in this case hip-hop and garage. The taking of 'everything but the burden' of Black music, to quote the title of one of Greg Tate's books (2003), and related to the trope of the 'white man who stole the blues' (Shank, 2001). There is also a history of white racist fandom of music in Britain that was ironically more culturally hybrid, such as skinheads listening to ska, American soul, and Jamaican rocksteady (Back, 2002).

While Skinner is working within multicultural contexts such as the UK garage scene, his whiteness offers him a level of privilege that helped him to break through the mainstream. A line from the song 'White America' by Eminem is relevant here: 'If I was Black, I would have sold half.' In other words, within this systemic framework, he was able to open doors for himself and others. This also includes others who would be said to tout the 'chav' stereotype, such as singers Lily Allen and rapper Lady Sovereign. The next section focuses on this ripple of influence, showing how Skinner's debut album was important not only for himself but for also the emergence of other English popular music artists, including singer-songwriters, R&B inflected pop, and grime.

9 Mainstreaming British Popular Music in the Twenty-First Century

As with So Solid Crew for grime, I argue that Mike Skinner's success helped to expand, if not open, doors to certain mainstream British popular music styles. He was by no means a sole catalyst, but I would argue that his international success played a part in supporting other new British artists on the global stage. The fact that home-grown British artists in the realm of urban music were substantial on the international and national stage meant that more support could and did follow. *Original Pirate Material* was released five months before the launch of BBC 1Xtra on August 2002, which, despite criticism of the ghettoization of certain artists at the BBC, created a space for 'urban' artists to share their material to a wider audience. Skinner was influenced by Black artists on pirate radio and the BBC and pirate stations that went legal were capitalizing on the success of artists who got their first airplay through the pirate radio medium. Rising critical acclaim is further documented as *OPM* was nominated for a Mercury Prize that year, losing to R&B singer and rapper Ms. Dynamite.[50] The following year, Dizzee Rascal won the prize for his major label debut *Boy in da Corner* (2003). Skinner is therefore part of a wider trajectory that illustrates the start of an increasing platform for British urban-inflected artists into the mainstream.

Ben Thompson, who put *OPM* as the number 1 album of that decade, writes that 'Original Pirate Material gave British rap an authentic new voice and provided the link between the Kinks and Dizzee Rascal' (Thompson, 2009). At the same time, grime was evolving in parallel and becoming independent of the UK garage culture, and Skinner gained from this scene as well. The success of *OPM* therefore helped to expand the platform for developments in grime and other home-grown localized English pop artists (such as Lily Allen and Adele). The album can be seen as an important link in the chain of development for 2000s and 2010s British popular music. While I would not make the case that UK localism or regionalism began with Skinner (I've mentioned The Kinks, Pulp, Ian Drury, and others earlier on), I would argue that he helped usher in (along with grime) a new wave of UK acts that celebrated the regional in different ways, and received national and international attention in part for doing so. These artists represented a generation now called 'elder millennial' (born 1980–1985) and 'millennial' (b. 1981–1996) of which Skinner was just outside the cusp of as he was born in 1978. For white English artists in particular, Skinner's 'chav'-like persona could be said to be in a lineage with artists releasing albums a few years after Skinner's debut such as Amy Winehouse, Lily Allen, and Plan B.

In 2002, the UK singles chart consisted of a mix of UK boy and girl bands (Girls Aloud, Westlife, Atomic Kitten, Sugababes), pop singers such as Gareth Gates and Will Young, Oasis, DJ Sammy, Daniel Bedingfield, and American artists such as Christina Aguilera, Eminem, Pink, Aaliyah, and Nelly. This mix of American R&B, rap, and UK pop and dance music would dominate for a few years, but I would argue that the rise of grime (e.g. Dizzee Rascal) and other English pop acts (e.g. Lily Allen, Katy B) would help contribute to an even more healthy home-grown music scene and its commercial success. The bigger success of Skinner's second album *A Grand Don't Come for Free* (released May 2004) is a part of a further development of British urban or urban-influenced pop artists who thrived from 2006 to 2008.

---

[50] It is worth noting that the Ms. Dynamite album sold single platinum, whereas *OPM* sold double.

Within commercial UK music, many artists were influenced by Black music but did not come from a Black British background themselves. The success of artists like Amy Winehouse, Lily Allen, Kate Nash, Plan B, and bands like the Arctic Monkeys seem to bear traces of Skinner's influence, elements of the working-class stereotypes recounted in lyrical stories and Skinner's regional accent. Journalist Caspar Llewellyn Smith writes in 2011, 'there is little disputing that, without The Streets, the charts today would look different – his influence on the confessional pop of the likes of Lily Allen as considerable as it is obvious on a new breed of UK rappers such as Plan B' (Smith, 2011). These artists had regional accents, told local tales, and became highly successful. While *OPM* predates MySpace, one could argue that MySpace became another tool in suggesting these DIY artists like Arctic Monkeys, Kate Nash, and Lily Allen (or their personae), were 'of the people'.[51] Allen and Nash are iconographic of the urban working-class girl, with elements of the aforementioned 'chav' stereotypes. Allen's pop music also suggested those Black Atlantic influences in a similar way to Skinner, her hit 'Smile' with the reggae-like upbeats reminiscent of 'Let's Push Things Forward', and 'LDN', painting a picture of London urban life, while sampling Tommy Cook and the Supersonics version of 'Reggae Merengue'.

The indie rock band Arctic Monkeys' debut album *Whatever People Say I Am, That's What I'm Not* was released in January 2006. The debut told stories of life in England, late-night drinking and trying to 'pull' women. While one might make more direct comparisons with bands like Blur, Pulp, and earlier The Kinks and The Beatles, journalists did compare the group's focus on English life to The Streets. One retrospective wrote, 'the young four-piece were variously described as the sound of young Sheffield, Yorkshire's answer to the Streets, and the first internet superstars' (Boden, 2009). Reviews mention the refusal to tone down their local dialect, and that the realistic depiction of domestic rows might make Britain's male population 'grimace' (Petridis, 2006). Lead singer Turner described his style as 'on a tightrope between Mike Skinner and Jarvis Cocker' (quoted in Monroe, 2022).

One rapper who performed white working class-ness in a similar vein to Skinner, but came out of the grime scene, was Lady Sovereign. According to Lily Allen, it was Lady Sovereign that suggested Allen put her music on MySpace. With EPs *Vertically Challenged* in 2005 and *Blah Blah* in 2006, her music reached the attention of labels across the pond, and eventually became the

---

[51] A review of Kate Nash in 2007 reads: 'Kate Nash, the internet-launched, Lily Allen-endorsed auburn-haired "yoof-queen," also starting a UK tour ... 20-year-old Nash certainly has her limitations, sounding far too often like (very weak) Smiths meets (derivative) Streets via Tracey Ullman circa her unlamented pop star period' (no author, 'The battle of the barnets', 2007).

first white British MC to be signed to an American label. Signed to Island Def Jam, with rapper Jay-Z as its president, she released the album *Public Warning* in 2006. In fact, at twenty-one years of age, she was the first non-American woman signed to the label. Simon Price writes, 'Back home, though, she is widely dismissed as a chavette novelty act' (Price, 2007), but some of the Englishness which felt exotic to US listeners with The Streets was also a key feature of Sovereign's signing and the push towards that market. She was the first ever British artist to hit the No. 1 chart spot on MTV America's TRL (Total Request Live) show, and toured the US in January 2007, supporting Gwen Stefani's show alongside Akon (Dotiwala, 2007). Sovereign emerged from the London grime scene, but perhaps was depicted vis-à-vis the stereotypes about British people through an American lens. Michel Sia reviews a 2006 performance by Skinner with reference to Sovereign:

> It is funny to recall that when Mr. Skinner's brilliant debut, 'Original Pirate Material,' arrived in 2002, he was touted as the next Eminem. That, obviously, was not to be. Back then who could have predicted that the first white British MC to land a huge deal with a leading American rap label would be a woman: a scrappy munchkin who disses fake tans in a West Indian accent? (That would be the entertaining opening act, Lady Sovereign; Jay-Z signed her to Island Def Jam and her full-length album is due this fall.) (Michel, 2006, P. E3)

The suggestion here is that Skinner helped to make such an internationalization possible. I would also take this further in the timeline to artists like Adele (debut album in 2008) who continue the social realism of these aforementioned artists while moving it into even more confessional singer-songwriter territory. One writer goes as far to say that the three figures of Allan, [Amy] Winehouse, and Adele defined the British female pop sound of the noughties (O'Flynn, 2018), and one can see Adele increasing her influence well into the 2010s. A parody of Adele by Katy Brand has the faux Adele singing, 'Every day I thank the Lord for what the BRIT School taught me/ embrace your chav like Lily does and don't end up like Amy/ So if you see me interviewed on T4, don't be surprised if I'm talking like an East End whore'.[52] From 2012, this video points to the disjunct between her strong Tottenham (North) London accent in her speaking voice, and the more soulful singing voice which has less trace of the accent. Interestingly, in the parody, she does a spoken verse which might as well come right out of the Mike Skinner playbook (it wouldn't have been odd to hear him do the same lyrics and delivery, especially as the Terry character from 'The Irony of it All'). By the second spoken verse she is selling fruit, selling

---

[52] https://www.youtube.com/watch?v=qKEGkC7hgQQ.

newspapers on the street corner, imitating football fans, and various stereotypes of the white male working-class geezer who is conservative minded politically ('Boiler packed it, has it? That's what you get if you pay Polish prices'). In a very short span of time, Brand covers a range of white male British London working-class stereotypes and characters which create humour through incongruity with Adele's voice and looks. It's a brand of masculinity touted by both Skinner and Arctic Monkeys and depicted in British soap operas. We could also point to spoken word artists like Kae Tempest and their album *Everybody Down* (2014) for constructing a narrative with characters who carry a story over the course of an entire album, akin to Skinner's second album *A Grand Don't Come for Free* (2004).

Skinner's positive reception in late 2000s grime and beyond has been demonstrated in interviews with artists like Lady Leshurr, Kojey Radical, and Chip who featured the 'Has It Come to This' beat on a 'School of Grime Remix'. Grime as a genre owes a lot to both hip-hop and UK garage, and they all reflect some of the more multicultural scenes in the UK (de Lacey, 2023). As a 'grandchild of the Windrush generation' (Boayke, 2017, p. 55) grime and most of its practitioners were Black British, and audiences were a broad mix, especially in centres like London and Birmingham. Caspar Melville notes,

> grime draws on deep familial, cultural and aesthetic connections to sound system, funk, rave and garage. And as with reggae, garage and jungle, though the majority of the producers of the music are black (though not all of them), the grime audience, both in London and that built globally through the internet, is decidedly multi-cultural (there is even a passionate grime scene in Japan). (Melville, 2019, p. 239)

Rather than a lineage, it was overlapping urban multicultural contexts in the late 1990s which gave rise to both grime and The Streets. And while So Solid Crew's proto-grime predates The Streets, Skinner's success did help the support for urban genres nationally and internationally while absorbing some of the market share.

Grime emerged in the early 2000s London, out of darker UK garage sounds. Pirate radio shows were important, and collectives of MCs became more prominent on radio shows. So Solid Crew (on Delight FM), Heartless Crew (on Mission), and Pay As U Go (on Rinse FM) would help yield what has now become known as grime. Some early examples of these proto-grime sounds include Pay As U Go's 'Know We' or So Solid Crew's 'Dilemma', both from 2000. Grime is often considered to start with 'Eskimo' by Wiley (2002), who called the new genre 'eskibeat', and 'Pulse X' by Youngstar

(2002). Boayke considers 2002 to be 'year zero' for grime, coming out of the pirate radio stations of London in particular. Like Skinner's music, grime came out of people's bedrooms, inspired by pirate radio, with a DIY approach to production technology. Grime was around 140 bpm like UK garage before, and perhaps not coincidentally the default tempo on the FruityLoops beat-making software (Hancox, 2018, p. 67; see also DJ Target, 2019).

The style was known by several names initially, including 8-bar (meaning eight-bar verse patterns), nu shape (which encouraged more complex 16-bar and 32-bar verse patterns), sublow (being a reference to the very low bassline frequencies), as well as eskibeat before it was solidified as grime when it was mainstreamed in 2003–2004. I have mentioned Dizzee Rascal's Mercury Prize for *Boy in Da Corner* in 2003 which gave some mainstream recognition, and grime had a large resurgence at the middle of the 2010s where we see Stormzy, JME, Skepta, and others achieving national and international fame. Grime has been at the BBC Proms, on the BRIT awards, and international tours as one of the most vibrant forms of Black British music in existence. Birmingham-based grime artist and 2010s viral video sensation Lady Leshurr discusses the influence Skinner had on her early development:

> [Skinner] always will be a legend in my eyes. Especially coming from [my hometown] Birmingham where we've always been mocked because of our accent. He was the first MC from up north to pave the way for the rest of the Brummy MCs that came after him. He used his real accent – the way he rapped was special because it was basically just talking on the track. Like spoken word with an instrumental. Genius. (Quoted in Myers, 2017)

UK artist Kojey Radical writes, 'I remember hearing [*Original Pirate Material*] for the first time and thinking, *This feels like the perfect medium between garage culture and indie music*' (Roy, quoted in Myers, 2017). And there is also a tangible link with mid-2000s grime via the 'School of Grime (The Streets Remix)' where grime rapper Chip raps with early figures in the genre such as D Double E and Jammer over a loop of 'Has it Come to this?' It has the feel of a UK garage breakbeat, no doubt used as an instrumental for grime freestyles at the time the album came out, and now a signifier of being 'schooled' in the history of the genre.[53] Jammer, who is featured on the remix, had said the following of *OPM*:

> It's one of the U.K. blueprint albums. That album could never be created again, that's why we are talking about it now. It's funny: Mike said to me one time at

---

[53] A subsidiary of 679 Recordings, Skinner's own record label The Beats was home to British hip-hop acts such as the Mitchell Brothers, Example and Professor Green.

a party that I was a big inspiration to him. I love the fact that he is still seeking inspiration from the people that seek inspiration from him. (Myers, 2017)

He also says, 'Grime emerged because we weren't really a part of garage. Garage was the club-driven beat music before grime in the U.K. – but *Original Pirate Material* showed a change in that. A lot of sounds and ways of putting records together were taken from that Mike Skinner album; everyone was inspired by it and took pieces from it' (quoted in Myers, 2017). The beat of 'School of Grime' most explicitly notes this linkage between the UK garage hybrids of Skinner and grime as a stylistic cousin of UK garage and US hip-hop.[54]

10 The Afterlife of *OPM* and The Streets

Skinner was contracted by his label to produce five albums as The Streets, and he did just that. After *OPM*, *A Grand Don't Come for Free* (2004) was even more successful, 4xPlatinum (1.2 million units) in the UK alone, with the largest hit from the album 'Dry Your Eyes' debuting at number one on the single charts in the UK. The final three albums, *The Hardest Way to Make an Easy Living* (2006), *Everything is Borrowed* (2008), *Computers and Blues* (2011) were not as commercially successful or as critically acclaimed as the first two but were solid offerings in a similar vein. In 2011, Skinner announced that the fifth album would be his last. He explained that he had 'run out of new avenues' with The Streets persona, but had also recently had a daughter in 2009 and was diagnosed with M.E. (Myalgic Encephalomyelitis aka Chronic Fatigue Syndrome) in 2008 (as discussed on the song 'Trying to Kill M.E.' on *Computers and Blues*). He states in a long *Guardian* interview that 'I've been doing [The Streets] for too long ... I should have moved on a long time ago' (Smith, 2011).

After Skinner retired as The Streets in 2011, he moved on to other projects, including films, and helped expand his independent record label (The Beats) which he co-founded in 2005 with Ted Mayhem. Skinner launched a new recording project called the D.O.T. in 2012 with Rob Harvey. He also collaborated with rapper Murkage Dave on a supergroup called Tonga Balloon Gang that organized club nights called Tonga. In 2012 he co-wrote his autobiography *The Story of the Streets* with Ben Thompson. He also co-produced several rap music documentaries for Vice magazine: *Hip-Hop In the Holy*

---

[54] Radio DJ Annie Mac said, 'Last year, we did a discussion feature for my radio show on BBC Radio 1 with Laurie from Slaves, Matty from The 1975, and Little Simz. All of them cited Mike Skinner as one of their biggest influences. The album is a bona fide classic, and it's still reverberating through popular music and influencing our U.K. artists left right and center.' Quoted in Myers (2017).

Land (2015), *Don't Call it Road Rap* (2017) about London drill, and *The Unstoppable Rise of Birmingham Rap* (2018). In the latter he praises the Walsall-based soul singer Jorja Smith whose music video to 'Blue Lights' (2018) features Skinner drinking tea and doing the washing up alongside footage of prominent Birmingham rappers and other figures from the region. Smith makes use of Skinner's 'everyday' persona reminiscent of the 'Don't Mug Yourself' video, and in hearing a song like Smith's 'On my Mind' (with Preditah) also shows a linkage (or nostalgia) to 2-step garage of almost two decades earlier.

Despite the retirement announcement in 2011, The Streets did return in various guises. Island Records released a mixtape entitled *None of Us Are Getting out of This Life Alive* in 2020. It was very much a vehicle for young stars to have guest spots (Jonze, 2020). This testifies to Skinner's artistic approach to support younger talent and to provide mentorship for them. The fifteenth anniversary of *OPM* offered Skinner the opportunity to take stock of his rich musical career and announced that his first two albums would be reissued on double vinyl in March 2018. Most recently, in October 2023, Skinner has released an album and a feature length film, both titled *The Darker the Shadow the Brighter the Light*. The film and 15-track album exist as a pair, as the album provides both soundtrack and narration that complements the film, a murder mystery set against the backdrop of London's club scene.

The passage of time has made some of those initial US-based reviews dated, and some reviewers have even provided their own reappraisals of *OPM*. In 2017, for example, music critic Rob Mitchum has made an apology for his ill-conceived review of *OPM* fifteen years earlier, asserting that the song has aged a lot better than those clueless reviewers such as himself:

> In 2002, the nuances of British electronic and hip-hop culture went way over your typical American music critic's head – which is my ****[55] excuse for wildly misinterpreting *Original Pirate Material* when reviewing the album for Pitchfork that year. Since then, we've had grime and dubstep to put U.K. garage in retrospective context. But I was pleased to discover Original Pirate Material still sounds bonkers 15 years later ... there's no way these combinations of beat and flow should work, but they do. Mike Skinner was also ridiculously adept at mixing the grand and the mundane, with severe, ragged orchestra loops scoring the most minute of observations ... Call it first-timer luck or genius, but The Streets's sound aged a lot better than its genre labels and clueless reviewers. (Quoted in Myers, 2017)

---

[55] I choose not to re-print the ableist slur that the journalist uses in the quote above, and therefore have censored it.

Above anything, such a reassessment shows the importance of looking at contemporary reviews to theorize the frames in which albums are read (and misread), and the importance of studying them with a historical and critical distance.

In the third UK lockdown during the coronavirus pandemic in 2021, Skinner started working on a track entitled 'Who's Got the Bag (21st June)'. The song celebrated the return of clubbing which was supposed to happen at the end of social contact restrictions on 21 June (Mixmag staff, 2021). The track is a repetitive edm-style club track, and in his wordplay style, riffs on the names of various government cabinet members: 'Tooting on the Boris, smoking on the Rishi, shooting with my hand cocked [Hancock]' – at the time Prime Minister Boris Johnson, Chancellor of the Exchequer Rishi Sunak and Health Minister Matt Hancock. It is arguably reflective of the entire country having been forced to become bedroom producers, trying to make art and stay sane in a challenging time while government officials mistreated self-imposed COVID rules by gathering for secret parties.

The single entitled 'Brexit at Tiffanys' (2022) featured the free-flowing stream of consciousness style we have grown accustomed to in Skinner's work. Part of a three-track release, 'Brexit at Tiffanys' featured the vocals of Jazz Morley and was metaphorically about a messy breakup. An accompanying music video continued with some of the more flag waving nationalist themes, union jack flags flying next to a tower block, which then cuts to Skinner in a café. Perhaps referencing the 'plenty of fried egg and tomato' of 'Don't Mug Yourself', he's sipping tea out of a union jack mug, having an English breakfast of fried egg, tomato and toast. The video contains images of London, the Queen, himself riding the iconic red bus, having fish and chips and beer, and Skinner discussing being 'Nostalgic for glamour that never happened'. This visual language of the video suggests a particular loneliness. We get the sense that his love will not meet him at Tiffany's like he wants ('Meet me on Bond Street, Brexit at Tiffanys'). His voice sounds laboured, almost drunk, slurring words, and talking slowly. This lyrical delivery may be metaphorical to the brokenness of 'Broken Britain': post-Brexit political instability mixed with post-COVID fatigue and exhaustion. The logo of The Streets, which has always been brandished on a small lighter, has now been refurbished as a lighter with a Union Jack on it. The white masculine vulnerability of *OPM* has somehow transformed into signifying tiredness, his brand (and persona) now updated as the performance of adulthood, tired and increasingly aware of one's mortality. Skinner may still be the voice of his generation, but that voice is growing weary with age.

The YouTube comments below the video speak to a nostalgia for an earlier time when Mike Skinner's voice was a soundtrack to a different time in their lives, a sentiment I can certainly share. User Mike Arnold writes for instance, 'Laying in bed not feeling great, I've just found this, and suddenly I'm transported back to a time when Mike Skinner's music made me feel things I've never felt before. I could cry listening to this song. I don't know why? But I just could . . . thank you Mr Skinner.'

Skinner's ability to bring back memories transcends linguistic and cultural boundaries. It is captured by the German indie rock group Kraftklub, for example.[56] In April 2022, they released their new album *Kargo* which included the single 'Ein Song reicht' ('One Song Is Enough'), which opens with the following chorus:

> Verdammter Mike Skinner
> Kate Nash, Lykke Li
> Tame Impala, The Killers
> Florence + the Machine
> Ich hab' mich wirklich angestrengt
> Alte Bilder abgehangen, dein'n Account deabonniert
> Die Erinnerung verdrängt
> Und ich hab' mir eingeredet, dass es funktioniert
> Aber ein, zwei Bands
> Die mich andauernd an die Zeit mit dir erinnern
> Tut mir leid für die Fans
> Aber die müssen leider jetzt aufhör'n für immer
> Immer wieder Mike Skinner

Translated to English:

> Damned Mike Skinner
> Kate Nash, Lykke Li
> Tame Impala, The Killers
> Florence + the Machine
>
> I have been really trying hard, takin´ down the old pictures,
> unsubscribing your account, suppressing memories
> Have been talking to myself that it works
> but one or two bands
> constantly remind me of the time with you
> I am sorry for the fans!
> But they sadly have to quit playing forever
> Always again Mike Skinner

[56] My sincere thanks to Sina Nitzsche for telling me about this song, and for helping with the English translation.

The protagonist in this break-up song is trying to forget his ex-girlfriend. Songs like those from Skinner, Kate Nash remind him of this partner. In order to get over the break-up, the protagonist does not want to play them anymore, but he does not manage to do that as he continues to listen to Mike Skinner who he likes and who reminds him of his girlfriend. The song translates Skinner's notion of white male vulnerability to an (East) German cultural context. Kraftklub, which started playing together in 2009, are audibly influenced by Skinner. They combine indie rock with spoken-style rap delivery over their music. Kraftklub are from Chemnitz in former East Germany (Erbacher and Nitzsche, 2017), and the black-and-white music video shows a deindustrialized landscape not dissimilar to England's Birmingham.

I point out this German example to show one example of non-Anglophone reception of English culture, and that the influence of Skinner and artists like him were prominent even in non-Anglophone countries. As early as 2002, Christian Hopwood writes in a review of the album that 'a small book could, and probably will, be written examining what The Streets has achieved with the execution *of Original Pirate Material*' (Hopwood, 2002). Now, twenty years after the album's release, I hope to have provided a substantial study of the album in the form of this Element. In a current era where so much of popular culture is looking backwards to reboots, retro, or nostalgia, the re-emergence of The Streets is hardly surprising. Whatever the motivations to revisit the album, twenty years on, there are multiple reminders that the status of *OPM* is one of a classic album.

Conclusion

This study has proposed an album-based framework for popular music analysis that breaks down the album into thematic elements. *Original Pirate Material* demonstrates a microcosm of urban male youth culture in turn-of-the-century England. Issues of nationhood, identity, and masculinity have gained new significance following Britain's departure from the European Union in 2021. Questions around Englishness (and Britishness) and the acknowledgement of both the history of Empire and the nation's status post-Empire has become even more urgent considering these political negotiations. These issues are reflected in the spatial politics of the album cover's visual language: the London tower block cover has taken on new meaning in the wake of the June 2017 Grenfell Tower fire, in ways that intersect with hyper localization, inequality, and social justice. *Original Pirate Material* demonstrates the potential for rap music to tell the everyday stories and feelings of some of its less visible and underprivileged citizens, even if these are fictionalized tales. These stories are politically relevant while also being sites of pleasure and comfort for its listeners, a feat that the most effective popular music can achieve.

This Element offers a more comprehensive understanding the complex interactions of musical cultures manifest on the album than previously published. The album's hybridity is achieved through convergences of genre, the local, the Black Atlantic, intertexts, technology, and ideologies around creativity and storytelling. It challenges perceived ideas of originality and authenticity, and operates in a long tradition of piracy, colonialism, and appropriation. Like the spirit of the album, this Element provides a multilogue of ideas, hyperlink-style references, and influences (including white masculinity, technology, intertextuality, the Black Atlantic, and everyday Englishness) in order to reveal more about *OPM* and its place within English popular culture as well as its meanings for international audiences.

As a musical artefact, *OPM* exists at a historical and cultural crossroads: between the US and UK-based trends, between garage and hip-hop genres, the physical and digital, the sampled and the new, the everyday and the global, and the expansion of British popular music styles under the optimism and social challenges of the New Labour Government. It is a key artefact at the dawn of twenty-first-century musical practice, one whose place in British popular culture is as formidable as it is influential.

References

No author. 'Back to Black Album Review – Amy Winehouse'. *Pitchfork.com*. 28 March 2007. https://pitchfork.com/reviews/albums/10032-back-to-black/#:~:text=Fortunately%2C%20Winehouse%20has%20been%20blessed, knife%20twist%2C%20so%20be%20it.

No author. 'Original Pirate Material Review'. *PopMatters* (2002). www.metacritic.com/music/original-pirate-material/the-streets/critic-reviews, original review is 'page not found'.

No author. 'The Battle of the Barnets'. *theguardian.com*. 18 November 2007. www.theguardian.com/theobserver/2007/nov/18/featuresreview.review4?CMP=gu_com.

No author. 'Streets to Chav up Proms'. *gigwise.com*. 23 October 2008. https://www.clashmusic.com/news/streets-to-chav-up-proms/.

Adams, Ruth. '"Home Sweet Home, That's Where I Come from, Where I Got My Knowledge of the Road and the Flow from": Grime music as an expression of identity in postcolonial London'. *Popular Music and Society* 42/4 (2019): 438–455.

Alibhai-Brown, Yasmin. *Exotic England: The Making of a Curious Nation*. London: Portobello Books, 2015.

Alim, H. Samy. *Roc the Mic Right: The Language of Hip Hop Culture*. New York: Routledge, 2006.

Allen, Lily. *My Thoughts Exactly*. London: Blink, 2018.

Back, Les. 'Voices of Hate, Sounds of Hybridity: Black Music and the Complexities of Racism'. *Black Music Research Journal* 20/2 (2002): 127–149.

Bell, Adam Patrick. 'Trial-by-fire: A Case Study of the Musician-Engineer Hybrid Role in the Home Studio'. *Journal of Music, Technology & Education* 7/3 (2014), 295–312.

Berger, Maurice, Brian Wallis, and Simon Watson, eds. *Constructing Masculinity*. London: Routledge, 1995.

Bhabha, Homi K. *The Location of Culture*. London: Routledge, 1994.

Bhopal, Kalwant. *White Privilege: The Myth of a Post-Racial Society*. Bristol: Policy Press, 2018.

Billig, Michael. *Banal Nationalism*. London: Sage, 1995.

Blacker, Terence. 'British Humour Had Always Been in a Class of Its Own'. *The Independent Online*. 29 August 2006. www.independent.co.uk/voices/commentators/terence-blacker/terence-blacker-british-humour-has-always-been-in-a-class-of-its-own-413741.html.

Boakye, Jeffrey. *Hold Tight: Black Masculinity, Millennials & the Meaning of Grime*. London: Influx Press, 2017.

Boden, Sarah. 'Arctic Monkeys: Newcomers of the Decade'. *theguardian.com*. 29 November 2009. https://www.theguardian.com/music/2009/nov/29/arctic-monkeys-interview.

Brackett, David. *Categorizing Sound*. Berkeley: University of California Press, 2016.

Bradley, Lloyd. *Bass Culture: When Reggae Was King*. London: Penguin, 2001.

Bradley, Lloyd. *Sounds Like London: 100 Years of Black Music in the Capitol*. London: Serpent's Tail, 2013.

Bramwell, Richard. *UK Hip-Hop, Grime and the City: The Aesthetics and Ethics of London's Rap Scenes*. London: Routledge, 2015.

Bramwell, Richard and James Butterworth. '"I Feel English as Fuck": Translocality and the Performance of Alternative Identities through Rap'. *Ethnic and Racial Studies* 42/14 (2019): 2510–2527.

Bush, John. 'Original Pirate Material'. *Allmusic* (2002). www.allmusic.com/album/original-pirate-material-mw0000662618.

Caramanica, Jon. 'The Streets, "Original Pirate Material" (Vice)'. *Spin.com*. 21 July 2003. https://www.spin.com/2003/07/streets-original-pirate-material-vice/.

Carmichael, Emma. 'Someone Cut Off Adele's BRIT Awards Speech, So Adele Flipped Everyone Off'. *Gawker*. 21 February 2012. www.gawker.com/5887115/someone-cut-off-adeles-brit-awards-speech-so-adele-flipped-everyone-off.

Caruso, Andrea. 'Europe and the United States in the Counterculture Decade'. In *The Transatlantic Sixties*. Grzegorz Kose, Clara Junker, Sharon Monteith, and Britta Waldschmidt-Nelson, eds., 122–143. Berlin: Verlag, 2013.

Chapman, Robert. 'The 1960s Pirates: A Comparative Analysis of Radio London and Radio Caroline'. *Popular Music* 9/2 (1990): 165–178.

Chang, Jeff. *Can't Stop Won't Stop: A History of the Hip-Hop Generation*. London: Ebury, 2004.

Clatterbaugh, Kenneth. *Contemporary Perspectives on Masculinity: Men, Women, and Politics in Modern Society*. 2nd Ed. Boulder: Westview Press, 1997.

Cochrane, Bonnie. 'Weak Become Heroes: Original Pirate Material by the Streets Classic Album Review'. *Soundandvision.blog*. 20 April 2020. https://soundandvision.blog/2020/04/20/classic-album-review-original-pirate-material-by-the-streets/.

Connell, John and Chris Gibson. *Sound Tracks: Popular Music, Identity and Place*. London: Routledge, 2003.

Connor, Neil. 'Chavs King Comes Home'. *business-live.co.uk*. 4 March 2005, updated 31st May 2013. https://www.business-live.co.uk/economic-develop ment/chavs-king-comes-home-3998220.

Cooper, Leonie. 'The Streets' 10 Best Songs'. *NME*. 13 October 2017. www .nme.com/news/streets-10-best-songs-2148735.

Corner, Lewis. 'What Happened to the 8 Biggest MySpace Music Stars?'. digitalspy.com. 29 July 2015. https://www.digitalspy.com/music/ a660773/what-happened-to-the-8-biggest-myspace-music-stars/.

Covach, John and Andrew Flory. *What's That Sound: An Introduction to Rock and Its History*. 5th Ed. New York: W. W. Norton, 2018.

Davies, Hunter. *The Beatles: The Authorised Biography*. London: Ebury Press, 2009.

Dawdy, Shannon Lee and Joe Bonni. 'Towards a General Theory of Piracy'. *Anthropological Quarterly* 85/3 (2012): 673–699.

De Carvalho, A. Tomaz. 'The Discourse of Home Recording: Authority of "Pros" and the Sovereignty of the Big Studios'. *Journal on the Art of Record Production* 7 (2012). http://arpjournal.com/the-discourse-of-home-record ing-authority-of-%E2%80%9Cpros%E2%80%9D-and-the-sovereignty-of- the-big-studios/.

D'Errico, Mike. *Push: Software Design and the Cultural Politics of Musical Production*. New York: Oxford University Press, 2022.

De Lacey, Alex. '"Let Us Know You're Locked": Pirate Radio Broadcasts as Historical and Musical Artefact'. *Popular Music History* 12/2 (2019): 194–214.

De Lacey, Alex. *Level Up!: Live Performance and Creative Practice in Grime Music*. London: Routledge, 2023.

Denney, Alex. 'Amy Winehouse Back to Black'. *drownedinsound.com*. 20 July 2007. https://drownedinsound.com/releases/10846.

Diamond, Ross. 'Garage mechanics'. *Newstatesman.com*. 22 April 2002. www .newstatesman.com/node/155417.

DiPiero, Thomas. *White Men Aren't*. Durham: Duke University Press, 2002.

Dotiwala, Jasmine. 'Jasmine's Juice'. *voice-online.co.uk*. 13 February 2007. http://jasminedotiwala.co.uk/.

Erbacher, Eric and Sina Nitzsche. 'Performing the double rupture: Kraftklub, popular music and post-socialist urban identity in Chemnitz, Germany'. *International Journal of Cultural Studies* 20/4 (2017), 437–455.

Exarchos, Michail. *Reimagining Sample-based Hip Hop: Making Records within Records*. London: Routledge, 2024.

Floyd, Samuel. *The Power of Black Music*. New York: Oxford University Press, 1995.

Gates Jr., Henry Louis. *The Signifying Monkey: A Theory of Afro-American Literary Criticism*. Oxford: Oxford University Press, 1988.

Gilroy, Paul. *After Empire: Melancholia or Convivial Culture?* London: Routledge, 2004.

Gilroy, Paul and Les Back. 'The Sounds in the Streets – Paul Gilroy Talks to Les Back'. *Street Signs: Centre for Urban and Community Research Newsletter* 1/5 (2003).

Glynn, Paul. 'Mike Skinner: "Music Is Genuine Chaos"'. *BBC News*. 10 July 2020. www.bbc.co.uk/news/entertainment-arts-53262665.

Goldschmitt, K. E. 'Hybridity'. *Oxford Music Online*. https://www.oxfordmusiconline.com/grovemusic/display/10.1093/gmo/9781561592630.001.0001/omo-9781561592630-e-1002256796?rskey=yQvbnJ&result=1.

Griffiths, Dai. *Radiohead's OK Computer*. Bloomsbury 33 1/3 Series. New York: Bloomsbury, 2004.

Groenningsaeter, Anders Kile. 'Musical bedroom: Models of creative collaboration in the bedroom recording studio'. MA Thesis. Queensland University of Technology. July 2017.

Hagstrom Miller, Karl. *Segregating Sound*. Durham: Duke University Press, 2010.

Hall, Stuart. 'Old and New Identities, Old and New Ethnicities'. In *Culture, Globalization and the World-System*, Anthony D. King, ed. London: Macmillan, 1991, pp. 41–68.

Hancox, Dan. *Inner City Pressure*. London: William Collins, 2018.

Hans, Simran. 'How the Iconic Artwork of *Original Pirate Material* Made a Subtle Statement about London Life'. *The Fader*. 23 March 2017. www.thefader.com/2017/03/23/original-pirate-material-cover-rut-blees-luxemburg-interview.

Hari, Johann. 'Why I Hate Little Britain'. *The Independent*. 22 November 2005, www.independent.co.uk/voices/commentators/johann-hari/johann-hari-why-i-hate-little-britain-516388.html.

Harkness, Geoff. 'Get on the Mic: Recording Studios as Symbolic Spaces in Hip-Hop Culture'. *Journal of Popular Music Studies* 26/1 (2014): 82–100.

Hebditch, Stephen. *London's Pirate Pioneers: The Illegal Broadcasters Who Changed British Radio*. London: TX, 2015.

Higgins, Mark. PhD Thesis. University of Bristol, forthcoming, 2024.

Hind, John and Stephen Mosco. *Rebel Radio: The Full Story of British Pirate Radio*. London: Pluto Press, 1985.

Holt, Fabian. *Genre in Popular Music*. Chicago: University of Chicago Press, 2007.

Hopwood, Christian. 'The Streets Original Pirate Material Review'. *BBC Music*. 25 March 2002. www.bbc.co.uk/music/reviews/zfdp/.

Jackson, Andrea. 'A Guide to the Jubilee Singers European Tour Collection, 1873–1878'. *Fisk University Archives*. April 2004. www.fisk.edu/wp-con tent/uploads/2020/06/jubilee-singersarchiveseuropeantourcollection1873-1878.pdf.

Jackson, Reed. 'The Story of FruityLoops: How a Belgian Porno Game Company Employee Changed Modern Music'. *Noisey*. 11 December 2015. www.vice.com/en/article/rnwkvz/fruity-loops-fl-studio-program-used-to-create-trap-music-sound.

James, Malcolm. *Urban Multiculture*. London: Palgrave Macmillan, 2015.

Jazz Monroe, 'Sex, drugs and on the dole: The Streets' Original Pirate Material at 20' The Independent 25 March 2022, https://www.independent.co.uk/arts-entertainment/music/features/the-streets-original-pirate-material-skinner-b2043992.html.

Jones, Owen. *Chavs: The Demonization of the Working Class*. London: Verso, 2016.

Jonze, Tim. 'Mike Skinner: It's Not Cool to Be 40 in a Nightclub, Getting off Your Face. But It Happens'. *The Guardian*. 16 March 2020. www.theguar dian.com/music/2020/mar/16/mike-skinner-its-not-cool-to-be-40-in-a-night club-getting-off-your-face-but-it-happens.

Kaloterakis, Stefanos. 'Creativity and Home Studios: An In-Depth Study of Recording Artists in Greece'. *Journal on the Art of Record Production* 8 (2013). http://arpjournal.com/creativity-and-home-studios-an-in-depth-study-of-recording-artists-in-greece/.

Kimmel, Michael. *Angry White Men: American Masculinity at the End of an Era*. New York: Nation Books, 2013.

Klosterman, Chuck. 'Streets Smarts'. *New York Times*. 19 October 2003. P. M24.

Krims, Adam. *Rap Music and the Poetics of Identity*. Cambridge: Cambridge University Press, 2000.

Kronengold, Charles. *Living Genres in Late Modernity*. Berkeley: University of California Press, 2022.

Kumar, Krishnan. 'English and British National Identity'. *History Compass* 4/3 (2006): 428–447.

Kumar, Krishnan. 'Negotiating English identity: Englishness, Britishness and the future of the United Kingdom'. *Nations and Nationalism*. 16/3 (2010): 469–487.

Lexis and Dr. Love. 'UK Garage History & Family Tree: 20 Years of UKG!'. 2014 www.musicismysanctuary.com/the-history-of-the-uk-garage-family-tree.

Lockyer, Sharon. 'Dynamics of Social Class Contempt in Contemporary British Television Comedy'. *Social Semiotics* 20/2 (2010): 121–138.

Marcus, Alan P. 'Skiffle in the UK: The Indigenization of a Musical Genre'. *Journal of Cultural Geography* 37/2 (2020): 216–235.

McLeod, Kembrew. 'Authenticity within Hip-Hop and Other Cultures Threatened with Assimilation'. *Journal of Communication* 49/4 (1999): 134–150.

Melville, Caspar. *It's a London Thing: How Rare Groove, Acid House and Jungle Remapped the City.* Manchester: Manchester University Press, 2019.

Meyer, Felix, Paul Sacher Stiftung, Carol J Oja, Wolfgang Rathert, and Anne C Schreffler, eds. *Crosscurrents, American and European Music in Interaction, 1900–2000.* Cambridge, MA: Harvard University Press, 2008.

Michel, Sia. 'Music Review: Giving Vocal Cords an Endurance Test'. *New York Times.* 29 June 2006. P. E3. https://www.nytimes.com/2006/06/29/arts/music/29stre.html.

Mitchum, Rob. 'Review – *Original Pirate Material*'. *Pitchfork.* 22 August 2002. https://pitchfork.com/reviews/albums/7531-original-pirate-material/.

Mixmag staff, 'The Streets Release New Track 'Who's Got the Bag (21st June)'. *Mixmag.* 5 March 2021. https://mixmag.net/read/the-streets-whos-got-the-bag-21st-june-sesh-news.

Moll, Hannah. 'UK Garage: The 40 Best Tracks of 1995 to 2005'. *Mixmag.* 15 March 2019. https://mixmag.net/feature/40-best-uk-garage-tracks-released-90s-00s (accessed 29 September 2022).

Myers, Owen. 'Why the Streets's Original Pirate Material Still Matters, 15 Years On'. *The Fader.* 23 March 2017. www.thefader.com/2017/03/23/streets-original-pirate-material-15th-anniversary.

Negus, Keith. *Music Genres and Corporate Cultures.* London: Routledge, 1999.

O'Flynn, Brian. 'Lily Allen's new album signifies a millennial coming of age'. *iD. vice.com.* 12 June 2018. https://redef.com/author/58d55428de3437070ee148d9.

Osumare, Halifu. 'Beat Streets in the Global Hood: Connective Marginalities of the Hip Hop Globe'. *Journal of American Culture* 24 (2001): 171–181.

Partridge, Kenneth. 'Americans Were Bound to Hate the Streets' Original Pirate Material.' *A.V. Club.* 17 February 2015. https://www.avclub.com/americans-were-bound-to-hate-the-streets-original-pira-1798276954 (accessed 3 July 2015).

Petridis, Alex. 'Arctic Monkeys, *Whatever People Say I Am, That's What I'm Not*'. *theguardian.com.* 13 January 2006. https://www.theguardian.com/music/2006/jan/13/popandrock.shopping6.

Price, Simon. 'Mika, Berkeley Square, London – Lady Sovereign, Scala, London'. *theindependent.co.uk.* 11 February 2007. https://www.rocksback

pages.com/Library/Article/mika-berkeley-square-london-lady-sovereign-scala-london.

Pickering, Michael. *Blackface minstrelsy in Britain*. London: Routledge, 2008.

Raphael, Amy. 'Jumping for Joy in Nash-ville'. *theguardian.com*. 22 July 2007. https://www.theguardian.com/music/2007/jul/22/popandrock3.

Reynolds, Simon. *Energy Flash: A Journey through Rave Music and Dance Culture*. London: Picador, 1998.

Reynolds, Simon. 'MUSIC: The British Can't Rap, Haven't You Heard?' *New York Times*. 20 October 2002. P. A28. https://www.nytimes.com/2002/10/20/arts/music-the-british-can-t-rap-haven-t-you-heard.html.

Roberts, Vicky. 'Skinner Set to Feature in 'Chav: The Movie'. *gigwise.com*. 16 September 2004. https://gigwise.com/news/2788/.

Robinson, John. 'Review – Original Pirate Material'. *NME*. 12 September 2005, www.nme.com/reviews/reviews-the-streets-6170-317638.

Robinson, Sally. *Marked Men: White Masculinity in Crisis*. New York: Columbia University Press, 2000.

Rose, Stephany. *Abolishing White Masculinity from Mark Twain to Hiphop: Crises in Whiteness*. Lanham: Lexington Books, 2014.

Rose, Tricia. *Black Noise: Rap Music and Black Culture in Contemporary America*. Middletown: Wesleyan University Press, 1994

Sannah, Kelefa. 'Critics' Choice: New CD's: The Streets'. *New York Times*. 24 April 2006. P. E3. https://www.nytimes.com/2005/10/10/arts/critics-choice-new-cds.html.

Sanneh, Kelefa. 'Teen Spirit: Arctic Monkeys Observed in the Wild'. *nytimes.com*. 30 January 2006. https://www.nytimes.com/2006/01/30/arts/music/30monkeys.html.

Shadle, Douglas W. *Anonin Dvorak's New World Symphony*. New York: Oxford University Press, 2021.

Shank, Barry. 'From Rice to Ice: The Face of Race in Rock and Pop'. In *The Cambridge Companion to Rock and Pop*, Simon Frith, John Street, and Will Straw, eds., 256–271. Cambridge: Cambridge University Press, 2001.

Simpson, T. J. 'The Streets: Original Pirate Material (Vice/Atlantic)'. *The Music Box* 10/2. February 2003. www.musicbox-online.com/str-pir.html#axzz70W9EKJAL.

Skinner, Mike (with Ben Thompson). *The Story of the Streets*. London: Corgi Books, 2012.

Skues, Keith and David Kindred. *Pirate Radio: An Illustrated History*. Stroud: Amberly, 2014.

Slater, Mark. 'Timbre and Non-radical Didacticism in the Streets' "A Grand Don't Come for Free": A Poetic-Ecological Model'. *Music Analysis* 30/2–3 (2011): 360–395.

Smith, Caspar Llewellyn. 'Interview; Mike Skinner: Why I'm killing off The Streets'. *The Guardian*. 2 January 2011. www.theguardian.com/music/2011/jan/02/mike-skinner-streets-interview-computers-blues.

Smith, Paul, ed. *Boys: Masculinities in Contemporary Culture*. London: Routledge, 1996.

Strachan, Robert. *Sonic Technologies: Popular Music, Digital Culture and the Creative Process*. New York: Bloomsbury, 2017.

Stratton, Jon. 'Judge Dread: Music Hall Traditionalist or Postcolonial Hybrid'. *Contemporary British History* 28/1 (2014): 81–102.

Target, D. J. *Grime Kids: The Inside Story of the Global Grime Takeover*. London: Trapeze, 2019.

Tate, Greg. *Everything but the Burden: What White People Are Taking from Black Culture*. New York: Broadway Books, 2003.

Thompson, Ben. 'Albums of the Decade No. 1: The Streets – Original Pirate Material'. *The Guardian*. 29 November 2009. www.theguardian.com/music/musicblog/2009/nov/29/streets-original-pirate-material.

Thornton, Sarah. *Club Cultures*. London: Polity, 1995.

Till, Rupert. 'The Blues Blueprint: The Blues in the Music of the Beatles, the Rolling Stones, and Led Zeppelin'. In *Cross the Water Blues: African American Music in Europe*, Neil A. Wynn, ed., 183–202. Jackson: University Press of Mississippi, 2007.

Titmus, Stephen. 'Nightclubbing: Happy Days, London's Sunday Scene and the Birth of UK Garage'. 17 March 2014 https://daily.redbullmusicacademy.com/2014/03/nightclubbing-happy-days.

Tyler, Imogen. '"Chav Mum Chav Scum": Class Disgust in Contemporary Britain'. *Feminist Media Studies* 8/1 (2008): 17–34.

Tyler, Katherine. *Whiteness, Class, and the Legacies of Empire on Home Ground*. Basingstoke: Palgrave Macmillan, 2012.

Wald, Elijah. *The Dozens: A History of Rap's Mama*. Oxford: Oxford University Press, 2012.

Waltzer, Daniel. 'Independent Music Production: How Individuality, Technology and Creative Entrepreneurship Influence Contemporary Music Industry Practices'. *Creative Industries Journal* 10/1 (2017): 21–39.

Waltzer, Daniel. 'Toward an Understanding of Creativity in Independent Music Production'. *Creative Industries Journal* 1 (2021): 1–14.

Warren, Emma. 'The Birth of Rave'. *The Observer*. 12 August 2007. www.theguardian.com/music/2007/aug/12/electronicmusic.

Watkins, S. Craig. *Hip Hop Matters*. Boston: Beacon Press, 2005.

Welsh, April Clare. 'The Streets Announces 20th Anniversary Vinyl Edition of "Original Pirate Material"'. 25 March 2022. https://djmag.com/news/streets-announces-20th-anniversary-vinyl-edition-original-pirate-material.

Westfox, James. 'The Streets: Original Pirate Material'. *Drownedinsound.com*. 25 March 2002. https://drownedinsound.com/releases/2881/reviews/3436-the-streets-original-pirate-material.

White, Joy. *Terraformed: Young Black Lives in the Inner City*. London: Repeater Books, 2020.

White, Michele. *Producing Masculinity: The Internet, Gender, and Sexuality*. New York: Routledge, 2019.

Williams, Justin A. *Rhymin and Stealin: Musical Borrowing in Hip-Hop*. Ann Arbor: University of Michigan Press, 2013.

Williams, Justin A. 'Sampling, Intertextuality, Copyright'. In *The Cambridge Companion to Hip-Hop*, Justin A. Williams, ed., 206–220. Cambridge: Cambridge University Press, 2015.

Williams, Justin A. *Brithop: The Politics of UK Rap in the New Century*. Oxford: Oxford University Press, 2021.

Wilson, Michael John. 'Making Space, Pushing Time': A Sudanese Hip-Hop Group and Their Wardrobe-Recording Studio'. *International Journal of Cultural Studies* 15/1 (2012): 47–64.

Wolton, Alexis. 'Tortugan Tower Blocks? Pirate Signals from the Margins'. *Datacide*. 26 March 2011. https://datacide-magazine.com/tortugan-tower-blocks-pirate-signals-from-the-margins/.

Yancy, George. *What White Looks Like : African-American Philosophers on the Whiteness Question*. New York: Routledge, 2004.

Zubieri, Nabeel. *Sounds English: Transnational Popular Music*. Champaign: University of Illinois Press, 2001.

Acknowledgements

This Element was made possible in part through a grant from the AHRC (AH/ V002988/1) around 'The Fifth Element', and was in collaboration with the DFG, our equivalent in Germany. Sina Nitzsche, the original German PI on the project, was extremely helpful, as ever, in the earliest stages of this project. Sina, you are always a pleasure to work with.

The biggest thank you of all goes to Lilian Holland. Lily is a PhD student of mine, and I have taught them since they were an undergraduate here at University of Bristol. They were a research assistant on this project who went above and beyond in their research and insight on the project. Since then, we have collaborated on other projects, and am I extremely grateful for their research skills and support.

Many scholars and friends looked at various drafts of the manuscript: Carlo Cenciarelli, Steven Gamble, Jonathan Godsall, James McNally, Tim Summers, and Katherine Williams. My thanks to Rupert Till for his help and input in the early stages of planning and writing the project. Alex de Lacey read a full draft in a later stage of the project and helped saved me from a few embarrassing mistakes, and provided a lot of important insight into the subject matter.

Our departmental writing group as ever has been a wonderful support group of formidable scholars and humans: Genevieve Arkle, Lindsay Carter, Chloe Chang, David Dewar, Zach Diaz, Stim Gamble, Kate Guthrie, Sarah Hibberd, Marko Higgins, Lily Holland, Prof. Emma Hornby, Gillian Hurst, Monique Ingalls, Marcus Jones, Richard Jones, Asli Kaymak, Ivan Mouraviev, Maeve O'Donnell, Inka Rantakallio, Mariia Romanets, Tommaso Sabbatini, Shaena Weitz, Jack Williams, Matthew Williams, and Emily Wride.

I most gratefully thank Simon Zagorski-Thomas for taking this Element on as series editor, and to music editor for Kate Brett for her sensitivity and encouragement. Lastly, I'd like to thank Mike Skinner for his artistry which, without him, the following study would not have been possible.

Cambridge Elements ☰

Twenty-First Century Music Practice

Simon Zagorski-Thomas
London College of Music, University of West London

Simon Zagorski-Thomas is a Professor at the London College of Music (University of West London, UK) and founded and runs the 21st Century Music Practice Research Network. He is series editor for the Cambridge Elements series and Bloomsbury book series on 21st Century Music Practice. He is ex-chairman and co-founder of the Association for the Study of the Art of Record Production. He is a composer, sound engineer, and producer and is, currently, writing a monograph on practical musicology. His books include *Musicology of Record Production* (2014; winner of the 2015 IASPM Book Prize), *The Art of Record Production: an Introductory Reader for a New Academic Field* co-edited with Simon Frith (2012), the *Bloomsbury Handbook of Music Production* co-edited with Andrew Bourbon (2020), and the *Art of Record Production: Creative Practice in the Studio* co-edited with Katia Isakoff, Serge Lacasse and Sophie Stévance (2020).

About the Series

Elements in Twenty-First Century Music Practice has developed out of the 21st Century Music Practice Research Network, which currently has around 250 members in 30 countries and is dedicated to the study of what Christopher Small termed musicking – the process of making and sharing music rather than the output itself. Obviously this exists at the intersection of ethnomusicology, performance studies, and practice pedagogy / practice-led-research in composition, performance, recording, production, musical theatre, music for screen and other forms of multi-media musicking. The generic nature of the term '21st Century Music Practice' reflects the aim of the series to bring together all forms of music into a larger discussion of current practice and to provide a platform for research about any musical tradition or style. It embraces everything from hip-hop to historically informed performance and K-pop to Inuk throat singing.

Cambridge Elements ☰

Twenty-First Century Music Practice

Printed in the United States
by Baker & Taylor Publisher Services

Printed in the United States
by Baker & Taylor Publisher Services